Research Methods in Business Studies

Research Methods in Business Studies

A Practical Guide

Pervez N. Ghauri
*Professor of Marketing, Faculty of Management and Organization, University of
Groningen, the Netherlands*

Kjell Grønhaug
*Professor of Business Administration, Norwegian School of Economics and
Business Administration, Bergen, Norway*

Ivar Kristianslund
Professor of Statistics, Norwegian School of Management, Oslo, Norway

Prentice Hall

New York London Toronto Sydney Tokyo Singapore

First published 1995 by
Prentice Hall Europe
Campus 400, Maylands Avenue
Hemel Hempstead
Hertfordshire HP2 7EZ
A division of
Simon & Schuster International Group

Typeset in 10/12 pt Times
by MHL Typesetting Ltd

Printed and bound in Great Britain by MPG Books Ltd, Bodmin, Cornwall

---

Library of Congress Cataloging-in-Publication Data

Ghauri, Pervez N., 1948–
    Research methods in business studies : a practical guide / Pervez
N. Ghauri, Kjell Grønhaug, Ivar Kristianslund.
      p.   cm.
    Includes bibliographical references and index.
    ISBN 0-13-015710-4
    1. Management—Research. 2. Business—Research.   I. Grønhaug,
Kjell. II. Kristianslund, Ivar.
HD30.4.G49   1994
658—dc20   94-31964
                                              CIP

British Library Cataloguing in Publication Data

A catalogue record for this book is available from
the British Library

ISBN 0-13-015710-4 (pbk)

---

6 7 8 01 00 99

To: Tyaba, Kjellaug and Leikney

Contents

List of figures   xi

List of tables   xiii

1 Introduction   1

   1.1 Purpose   1
   1.2 Readership   2
   1.3 On the use of the book   4

2 Research in business studies   5

   2.1 Systematic research versus common sense   6
   2.2 Different research orientations   8
   2.3 Induction and deduction   8

3 Problem formulation and problem handling in (practical) research   11

   3.1 Wrestling with research problems   11
   3.2 The research process   13
       3.2.1   Conceptual (theoretical) and empirical level   15
       3.2.2   Research and knowledge   15
       3.2.3   What comes first: theory or research?   16
   3.3 Concepts: building blocks in research   17
   3.4 Models in research   19
       3.4.1   Model purposes   20
   3.5 Role of reviewing past literature   23
   3.6 Concluding remarks   24

4 Research designs   26

4.1 The design problem   26
4.2 Problem structure and research design   27
4.3 The problem of 'cause'   29
    4.3.1   The importance of theory   30
4.4 The classical experiment   31
4.5 Validity threats   33
4.6 Other research designs   35
    4.6.1   Cross-sectional designs   35
    4.6.2   Time series   37
    4.6.3   The one-shot case study   37
4.7 Requirements in research design   38
    4.7.1   Research and choices   39

5 Measurements: mapping the empirical world   41

5.1 Defining measurement   41
    5.1.1   Objects, properties and indicators   43
5.2 Levels of measurement   43
    5.2.1   Nominal level   44
    5.2.2   Ordinal level   45
    5.2.3   Interval level   45
    5.2.4   Ratio scale   45
5.3 Validity and reliability in measurement   46
    5.3.1   Multiple indicators   47
    5.3.2   Construct validity   48
    5.3.3   Other forms of validity   49
5.4 Improving your measurements   51
5.5 Measurements in 'qualitative' research   52

6 Data collection and sources   54

6.1 Secondary data   54
    6.1.1   Advantages of secondary data   55
    6.1.2   Disadvantages of secondary data   56
6.2 Primary data   57
    6.2.1   Observations   57
    6.2.2   Surveys and questionnaires   58
    6.2.3   Interviews   64
    6.2.4   Preparing for an interview   66
    6.2.5   Pre-interview   68
    6.2.6   The interview   69
    6.2.7   Post-interview   71

7 Sampling   73

7.1 Why take a sample? Basic concepts   73
7.2 Probability and non-probability sampling   73
7.3 Simple random sampling: an example   74
7.4 Stratified random sampling   77
7.5 Systematic sampling   78
7.6 Cluster sampling   79
7.7 Determining sample size   80

8 Qualitative methods   83

8.1 When to use qualitative methods   85
8.2 Types of qualitative method   86
  8.2.1 Historical review   87
  8.2.2 Group discussion   87
8.3 Case study method   87
  8.3.1 Preparing for a case study   89
  8.3.2 *A priori* propositions   90
  8.3.3 How to select the cases   90
  8.3.4 How to conduct a case study   91
  8.3.5 Different types of case study design   92
8.4 Triangulation   93
8.5 Analyzing qualitative data   95

9 Data analysis   97

9.1 Coding and storing your observations   97
9.2 The use of statistical software packages   99
9.3 Analyzing one variable   99
9.4 Cross-tabulation   102
9.5 Two-sample problems regarding population means   106
9.6 Simple linear regression   110
9.7 Multiple regression   114
9.8 Dummy variables in regression analysis   118
  9.8.1 Independent dummy variables   118
  9.8.2 Dependent dummy variable   121
9.9 Linear discriminant analysis   122
9.10 Principal components analysis   125
9.11 Factor analysis   128
9.12 Other methods of analysis   129

10 Writing the final report   132

10.1 Structure of the report   132
  10.1.1 Title page   133

10.1.2	Table of contents	133
10.1.3	Executive summary	134
10.1.4	Introduction and problem statement	134
10.1.5	Theoretical background	134
10.1.6	Methodology	134
10.1.7	Findings	135
10.1.8	Conclusions and recommendations	136
10.1.9	Footnotes	136
10.1.10	Bibliography or references	138
10.2	Form and style	139
10.3	Headings	140
10.4	Language and flow	140

References   141

Appendix A: Review of statistics   144

A.1	Basic terms	144
A.2	Probability distributions	145
A.3	Descriptive measures in the population	146
A.4	Joint distributions and related concepts	147
A.5	Independence	147
A.6	Models, parameters and assumptions	148
A.7	Describing the sample	150
A.8	Sampling and sampling distributions	152
A.9	Principles of statistical inference	153
	A.9.1 Introduction	153
	A.9.2 Computing confidence limits	154
	A.9.3 Testing hypotheses	154

Index   157

List of Figures

Figure 2.1	Induction and deduction	9
Figure 3.1	The research process	14
Figure 3.2	Production and use of theory	16
Figure 3.3	Operational definition of sales during a specific time interval	18
Figure 3.4	Organizational chart	21
Figure 4.1	The classical experiment	31
Figure 4.2	The one-shot case study	38
Figure 5.1	Mapping (assignment)	42
Figure 5.2	Measurement: the link between the conceptual and empirical levels	43
Figure 5.3	Object/phenomenon, properties and indicators	44
Figure 5.4	Seven-point scale	46
Figure 5.5	Measurement errors	47
Figure 5.6	Responses and sense-making	52
Figure 6.1	Sources of primary data collection	57
Figure 6.2	Choices for collecting primary data through observations	58
Figure 6.3	Planning a survey	59
Figure 6.4	Categories for closed questions	61
Figure 6.5	Scale for ranking answers	62
Figure 6.6	Examples of escape routes	63
Figure 6.7	A typology of interviews	65
Figure 8.1	The difference in emphasis in qualitative versus quantitative methods	84
Figure 8.2	Qualitative and quantitative methods and techniques	86
Figure 8.3	Basic designs for case studies	92
Figure 8.4	Components of data analysis: interactive model	96
Figure 9.1	Histogram of the data in Table 9.1	100
Figure 9.2	Scatter plot of CarSales against TV-Ads	111
Figure 9.3	Scatter plot and points on the regression line	114

Figure 9.4   Plot of data from Table 9.5   120
Figure 9.5   Plot of PC2 against PC1   127
Figure 10.1 Example of a table of contents   133

List of Tables

Table 3.1 Test marketing survey results   12
Table 4.1 Cross-table   29
Table 4.2 Covariation   30
Table 4.3 Reported improvement in the test and control groups   32
Table 4.4 The effects of message and gender   33
Table 4.5 Reading of advertisement and purchase   34
Table 4.6 Innovativeness by organizational size   36
Table 4.7 Control for 'third' variable   36
Table 5.1 Scales of measurement   44
Table 5.2 Two methods, two constructs   49
Table 7.1 Abbreviated example of a data matrix   76
Table 7.2 Typical sample sizes for studies of human and institutional
populations   82
Table 8.1 Methods of data collection to study managerial issues   95
Table 9.1 Car ownership per household in a random sample   99
Table 9.2 Cross-tabulation of two variables   102
Table 9.3 Cross-tabulation of three variables   103
Table 9.4 Data matrix   106
Table 9.5 Data including dummy variables   119

CHAPTER 1

Introduction

Facts do not simply lie around waiting to be picked up. Facts must be carved out of the continuous web of ongoing reality, must be observed within a specified frame of reference, must be measured with precision, must be observed where they can be related to other relevant facts. All of this involves methods.

(Rose, 1965: 11)

One of the most frustrating things for business students is writing theses and research reports. Students often have problems understanding the importance of theory and methodology in writing good business reports. This frustration is further enhanced due to the absence of a suitable text that they can use as a guide to methodology issues in their project work. The message of this book is that scientific methods are a question of consciousness and awareness, and should not be seen as difficult, strange or unnecessary.

Students need to understand the basic methodological approaches to management and business research. This understanding helps them in the initial stages of their thesis and project work, providing them with confidence and purpose. We do not intend to give students ready-made tools or advocate a particular approach to research in business studies. The idea is to let students understand that there is no 'best' method for business research and that the choice of method depends upon the research problem, the research design and the purpose for the research.

1.1 Purpose

The purpose of this book is to help students get rid of the myth that research is 'too scientific' and unnecessary in business studies. It is also intended to help them understand the language and approach of science and research. It will assist them in understanding how properly structured and argued reports can be more convincing and valid than reports based on a practical approach or common sense. In our opinion, a scientific approach and common sense have much in common. The scientific approach, however, is a more systematic and controlled treatment of common sense. A layperson uses theories and concepts but in a loose manner. Often, people accept whatever sounds consistent with their beliefs and values: an increase in unemployment is because of immigrants, etc. A scientific approach, on the other hand, systematically examines hypotheses before either believing or discarding them.

This book is designed to help students understand that a conscious (scientific) approach is the most appropriate for research and problem-solving projects. This means making students understand that before beginning research on a project, they must be aware of what they are doing and what they are not doing; they have to clarify for themselves and for the reader the perspective they have chosen, and they must identify who should benefit from the study. In other words, they must learn how to formulate a problem, how to choose a particular method and how to argue and motivate. They must also learn how to write a valid and reliable report, which is used for the purpose of research and for managers or decision-makers. We provide students and others involved in research and in business studies with clear, hands-on guidelines for doing research. The book will deal with the following:

- Explaining how to cope with problems.
- Explaining different types of research, the role of the researcher and the importance of methods and models.
- The practicalities of research, such as problem formulation, relating the research to previous studies, choosing a suitable methodology, presenting results, and finding and drawing conclusions.
- A discussion of different methods of data collection and analysis, qualitative as well as quantitative, and their advantages and disadvantages.
- How to test the assumptions necessary for the method and technique being used, and whether these assumptions are valid: in other words, validation of methods and models and not only validation of hypotheses.
- The practical issues around research in business studies, providing some practical guidelines for questionnaire development, interviewing and report writing.

1.2 Readership

This book is primarily meant for MBA, Master of Science and undergraduate students in Business Studies. In Europe, most schools and universities require their graduate as well as undergraduate students to write a thesis or a research report at the final stage of their studies. These students are the primary target for this text. Students often find the books available in the market either too general or too narrow, dealing with only one aspect of research, such as surveys, interviews, case studies or quantitative methods. This book, on the other hand, has an integrative approach and is especially adapted to research in business studies. The book will also be highly useful for consultants and business people working with research projects, problem solving and report writing. It is organized in the following way.

In Chapter 2 we discuss the meaning of research with a special reference to business studies. The focus here is to discuss the difference between research and practical problem solving or common sense. In Chapter 3 the role of theory in business research is discussed. Here the focus is on the research process and on the formulation of the research problem. It is our observation that most students of business studies face difficulties in formulating a research problem, and in differentiating between a research problem and a research topic. In this chapter we also discuss the importance of models and systematic thinking in research.

Chapter 4 deals with the research design and problems related to the choice of research design: how the research problem is and should be related to the design. Different types of research design are presented and their usage is discussed. Examples are used to illustrate the importance and relevance of research design. Problems related to validity and reliability are also dealt with in this chapter.

Chapter 5 handles the important problem of measurement and operationalization of research findings and data. Measurement of empirical research is a difficult task as the quality of information depends to a large extent upon the measurement procedures used in gathering and analyzing data. The chapter takes us through different types, levels and scales of measurement. Validity and reliability in measurement are particularly stressed. Some guidelines are provided to improve measurement, especially in qualitative research.

Chapter 6 deals with issues such as data collection, different types of data resources and what is meant by the right kind of data. Sources of secondary as well as primary data collection and their advantages and disadvantages are stated. Surveys and interviews are particularly discussed and step-by-step guidelines for conducting interviews are provided.

Chapter 7 deals with sampling, which is an important issue in business research. The chapter discusses different types of sampling technique and how we should go about drawing a sample. Some suggestions for storing and analyzing data are also given.

Chapter 8 takes up the difference between qualitative and quantitative research methods. The focus in the chapter is on qualitative methods. Issues such as when to use qualitative research methods and different types of qualitative method are discussed, particularly the case study method and when to use it. Guidelines on how to conduct case studies are provided. The chapter ends with some discussion on triangulation, where more than one methodology can be combined in the study of the same phenomenon.

Chapter 9 provides guidelines on and a practical demonstration of how to analyze data. Coding and storing of data and how to analyze different variables are discussed. A number of techniques, such as cross-tabulation, regression, usage of dummy variables, discriminant analysis and principle component analysis, and how these techniques can be used in business research, are presented. To this chapter an appendix is attached, partly to provide an insight into statistics for those who have less knowledge or who need to refresh their knowledge of statistics, and partly to explain some problems with measurement of population, sampling and statistical inference.

Finally, Chapter 10 provides guidelines for writing up a report. The process of writing up the final report is tiresome work. The report has to be concise, consistent and convincing. The writing style of the report is also important to convince the reader that the report is valid and reliable. In this chapter, the structure of the report is discussed from section to section with examples and illustrations. Guidelines for form and style, for usage of footnotes and bibliography are also provided.

1.3   On the use of the book

When working with the book, it is recommended that the reader first read the whole text. Before starting to work on the business research project, a thorough understanding of the role of theory in practical research and the objective of the research is needed (Chapter 3). When actually working on the research project, the reader should go back to the chapters relevant to the specific aspects of the researcher's problems, such as measurement problems or problems related to choosing adequate statistical tests.

CHAPTER 2

Research in business studies

If we have mentioned the actual results of investigation first, the reader could have labelled these obvious also. Obviously, something is wrong with the entire argument of obviousness. It should really be turned on its head. Since every kind of human reaction is conceivable, it's of great importance to know which reactions actually occur most frequently and under what conditions; only then will a more advanced social science develop.

(Lazarsfeld, 1959: 480)

The purpose of this chapter is to explain what we mean by research in business studies and to discuss differences between systematic research and common sense or practical problem solving. Different research orientations are also discussed to illustrate the influence of researchers' backgrounds and basic beliefs surrounding the research methods and processes. We believe that research papers or theses at the Masters level, when successfully completed, should demonstrate that the candidate can systematically handle and analyze a problem, arriving at valid conclusions. In other words, it is a professional training process through which students can learn to think and work systematically. The advantage of systematic thinking is that it contributes to accuracy and a more orderly approach in handling research or business problems.

The increasingly complex nature of business operations and decision making demands a systematic and thoughtful approach. The importance of research in business studies, in schools and in business has therefore increased. Practical problem solving and decision making are (or at least should be) becoming more and more similar to research. Economic and marketing research are common activities in medium-sized and larger companies. And most of the decision making in these companies is based on research.

> Research in business studies is not much different from practical problem solving.

2.1 Systematic research versus common sense

There is a common belief that research is an academic activity undertaken by researchers who are not at all familiar with managerial culture and the nature of problems faced by business managers. At the same time, several studies have revealed that managers do not know how to use research findings and thereby cannot utilize the results and conclusions of research (Whitley, 1984; Gill and Johanson, 1991). In our opinion, research in business studies and managerial problem solving are not much different from each other. Managers need to have some knowledge and evaluation capabilities to understand the consequences of their decisions. In other words, managerial decision making or problem solving, if done systematically, should lead to better decisions and results than those decisions made exclusively through intuition or personal likes and dislikes. Managers must have the capability to analyze their situations and to use investigative approaches to decision making and problem solving. The systematic procedures and approaches of advancing knowledge, suggested by the research process, also serve as a disciplined and systematic procedure for managerial problem solving.

As a first step, actors in both management and research activities need to decide what they want to achieve. This is followed by collecting relevant information and facts that can help in achieving the first objective. The information collected needs to be analyzed and put into a structure which helps to achieve a purpose or initiate different actions. This process — deciding what to do, collecting information, discarding irrelevant information, analyzing the relevant information and arriving at a conclusion/decision in a systematic procedure — is useful for cumulative knowledge as well as the personal development of the researcher and manager alike (Revans, 1971; Gill and Johnson, 1991).

The purposes of doing research are multiple, such as to describe, explain, understand, foresee, criticize and/or analyze already existing knowledge or phenomena in social sciences. The job of a researcher is often that of an observer and each observation is prone to error: therefore, we go out and research to find a better 'truth'.

> Research is different from common sense because it is done to achieve specific goals, relies on specific methods and is done systematically.

If the role of a researcher is that of an observer, then what is the difference between an observer who can draw conclusions with common sense and a researcher? The difference is that observations made by the researcher should be systematic, arguable and challengeable. The researcher explains to us how he/she collects information, argues for the results obtained and explains their limitations. In an ideal situation, if anybody else had made observations using the same methods, they would have come up with more or less the same results. The role of the researcher thus becomes very important. When we look and observe, we see differently depending upon our background and what we know and expect. Two different people observing the same object may see two different things. It is thus very important to discuss both the object and the observer and biases. For this reason, the observer has to explain and convince the reader of the purpose and methods of observation.

The usefulness of research is often discussed, especially when it comes to things that seem self-explanatory and clear through common sense. But the very same common sense and self-explanatory objects/beliefs may prove to be wrong through research. Common sense and beliefs, influenced by society and culture, provide us with a non-conscious ideology and we believe in things without being aware of the reality. As Bem (1979: 89) said, 'Only a very unparochial and intellectual fish is aware that his environment is wet.' This is further illustrated by the following example:

> A man and his son are involved in an automobile accident. The man is killed and the boy, seriously injured, is rushed to the hospital for surgery. But the surgeon takes one look at him and says, 'I am sorry, but I cannot operate on this boy. He is my son.' (Selltiz *et al.*, 1976: 4)

Whenever we tell this story to our students, the majority of them do not understand the catch. We unconsciously believe that a surgeon is always a man and therefore do not even consider the thought that the surgeon can be the mother of the boy.

Scientific research often challenges these non-conscious ideologies and beliefs by scrutinizing them. Challenging old beliefs, turning things upside down and creating new beliefs is not always comfortable. Research corrects our misbeliefs, generates new concepts and broadens our perspectives and perceptions. This is particularly true because research does all that which is beyond common sense — while common sense considers most things as given. The fundamental difference here is, as mentioned earlier, that research involves scientific methods. The conclusions drawn from research lead to new theories and beliefs. The general purpose of research, and it is one on which we hope everybody can agree, is to improve social life. In business research, the purpose is to understand how and why things happen. The research corrects our misbeliefs and provides new perspectives. At times it can be uncomfortable, as illustrated by the following example:

> A well-known scientist (some say it was Bertrand Russell) once gave a public lecture on astronomy. He described how the earth orbits around the sun and how the sun, in turn, orbits around the center of a vast collection of stars called galaxy. At the end of the lecture, a little old lady at the back of the room got up and said, 'What you have told us is rubbish. The world is really a flat plate supported on the back of a giant tortoise.' The scientist gave a superior smile before replying, 'What is the tortoise standing on?' 'You are very clever, young man, very clever,' said the lady, 'But it's turtles all the way down.' (Hawkins, 1988: 1)

The above discussion makes it clear that the difference between a scientific observation and a layperson's observation is that scientific research is done systematically and is based on logic and not beliefs: therefore, we stress a logical relationship.

2.2 Different research orientations

The research process and the research method used are influenced by the researcher's background when it comes to research orientation. A particular research orientation prescribes the relationship between the methods, data, theories and values of the researcher. Social knowledge builds one upon another. Scientific observations provide new theories, correcting, modifying, extending and clarifying the older and existing ones. Most methodology books describe 'originality' or 'original contribution to knowledge' as a basic condition for a scientific study. Although the demand for originality is perhaps the most controversial, its importance and meaning should not be misunderstood. Students normally believe that topics used by others in their theses should not be studied, because by doing so the students would lose originality. We believe 'originality' describes studies which create a new dimension to already existing knowledge. It implies that there is some novel twist, fresh perspective, new hypothesis or assumption, or new and innovative methods of handling an already existing topic/knowledge that makes the project a distinctive contribution. In business studies, it is equally possible or perhaps more useful to direct research projects towards more sharply delineated tasks.

The researchers do not preach or ask whether the social activity observed is good or bad; they just present and explain it. In fact, that is the starting point of research: we have a number of assumptions/speculations, but we should not accept or reject them unless we study their assumptions critically.

2.3 Induction and deduction

A researcher observes and faithfully records what is seen without any prejudice. Some of these statements of observation are established as true and serve as the basis for theories and laws. There are two ways of establishing what is true or false and of drawing conclusions: induction and deduction. Induction is based on empirical evidence, while deduction is based on logic.

Through *induction* we draw general conclusions from our empirical observations. This process goes from assumption to conclusion and is illustrated as follows:

- Assumption: Psychiatrists have found that psychological problems in patients depend upon their experiences in childhood.
- Conclusion: All psychological problems are based on experiences in childhood.

It is, however, important to note that we can never be 100 per cent sure about the above inductive conclusion, as the conclusion is based on some empirical observations. Sometimes, conclusions based on hundreds of observations can also be wrong.

This can be explained by the prognosis on election results in a political general election. Although the prognosis concludes that the Labour Party is going to win the election, we cannot be sure until we have seen the final results. In other words, we can arrive at more or less probable results, but not with 100 per cent certainty.

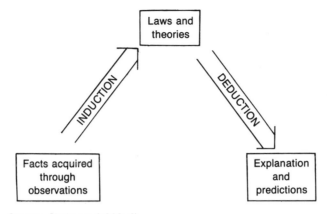

Source: Chalmers (1982: 6).

Figure 2.1 Induction and deduction

By *deduction* we mean that we draw conclusions through logical reasoning. In this case, it need not be true in reality, but it is logical. The process of deduction goes as follows:

- Assumption: All metals expand when heated.
- Assumption: Rail tracks are built of metal.
- Conclusion: Rail tracks will expand when heated.

The above examples explain the difference between induction and deduction. The difference is that facts acquired through observations lead us to theories and hypotheses, while with deduction (logical reasoning) we accept or reject the hypotheses. This acceptance and rejection then helps us to explain or predict (see Figure 2.1).

In the process of research, methods begin with ideas and facts which lead us to propositions, theories and predictions. New theories and predictions lead us to new ideas and facts, and a new cycle begins, leading us to new theories. When we utilize observed facts in generating a theory which is consistent with these facts, we are doing induction. In other words, induction is the process of observing facts to generate a theory and is perhaps the first step in scientific methods. While doing research we formulate propositions after observing the relationship between different variables of our study. Most researchers in business studies go through this method, observing facts which lead them to propositions and later to theories.

On the other hand, in deduction we look at the consequences of a theory. There is an established school of thought which believes that the entire research process is initiated by theories. Deduction involves the gathering of facts to confirm or disprove hypothesized relationships among variables that have been deduced from propositions or earlier theories.

As we can see, discussion about induction and deduction presents us with two alternative ways of building theories. Most researchers and scientists believe that they have been using both of these in their research. In both cases, however, a great deal of creativity and imagination is demanded from the researcher or investigator. Both induction and deduction demand that we go beyond statistical significance to systematic data collection, and that we are aware of the sensitive question of the relevance of data to theory or study. Moreover, both demand that the investigator keep up to date with theories and ideas and their relevance to scientific methods.

CHAPTER 3

Problem formulation and problem handling in (practical) research

He who loves practice without theory is like the sailor who boards ship without a rudder and compass and never knows where he may be cast.

(Leonardo da Vinci, 1452–1519)

Practical business research is often thought of as collecting data from various statistical publications, constructing questionnaires and analyzing data by using computers. Research, however, also compromises a variety of important non-empirical tasks, such as finding/'constructing' problems, and developing perspectives or models to represent the problem under scrutiny. In fact, such aspects of research are often the most crucial and skill demanding. The quality of the work done at the conceptual (theoretical) level largely determines the quality of the final empirical research. This is also the case in practical business research.

3.1 Wrestling with research problems

Research problems are *questions* that indicate gaps in the scope or the certainty of our knowledge. They point to problematic phenomena, observed events that are puzzling in terms of our currently accepted ideas, or current ideas that are challenged by new questions. Thus, research relates to questions to be answered, such as 'What is the size of the market?' and 'What is the effect (if any) of our advertising effort?'

(Practical) research is wrestling with problems. To answer (solve) a research problem, the researcher must be able to answer the following two questions:

1. What is the problem?
2. How should I proceed in order to solve the problem?

The questions seem trivial, but often this will not be the case. Answering the first question implies that the researcher really *knows what s/he wants to know*. A common

Table 3.1   Test marketing survey results

Household size	Total no. of households	Purchasing households
Large	200	50
Small	300	30
Sum	500	80

mistake is to go ahead with data collection and other 'practical' activities before knowing the problem. Such an approach often ends up in a situation where 'a bunch of data is searching for a problem' when time is out and money used.

A useful strategy to get hold of the research problem is to ask *questions*. Good questions have the following characteristics:

● They express relationship(s) between two (or more) variables.
● They are clear, i.e. what is asked is understood.

The advantage of expressing relationships between variables is that they can be tested. For example, a marketing manager wonders whether the marketing effort should be directed towards large or small households, depending on where the propensity to purchase the firm's product is the highest. A possible question is thus: 'Is there a relationship between household size and propensity to purchase?' Or, more specifically, 'Is it the case that large households are more likely to buy than small households?'

Note that in the above case the following two variables are included: household size and propensity to purchase. Given available data — for example, data gathered through test marketing in a specific area of household size — the hypothesis, i.e. the relationship expressed in the question, can be tested. Assume that a test marketing programme followed up by a survey study based on a random sample of the households gives the results shown in Table 3.1.

Here it is evident that the propensity to purchase, i.e. purchasing households/total number of households, is higher for large than for small households: $50/200 = 0.25$ and $30/300 = 0.1$, respectively, indicating that there is a positive relationship between size of household and propensity to purchase. This can also be tested statistically (see Chapter 9). Expressing relationships as in the above question (or hypothesis) allows *falsification*, which is at the heart of hypothesis testing.[1]

The initial research problem is often rather vague and general. For example, a small business manager has difficulty in understanding what influences the firm's performance in 'good' and 'bad' times. How can this ambiguous problem be approached? From cost accounting we know the following:

Profit = (Price − Variable costs) · Quantity − Fixed costs

Based on this simple equation (model), we may ask several questions, such as:

● Do the prices for the firm's product fluctuate?

- Does the firm use a specific raw material which fluctuates highly in price?
- Does the demand for the firm's product fluctuate?

By asking such questions, the problem can be narrowed down and the effort concentrated to solve the real problem. But there is more to it than this, such as: what initiates the questions? In the above examples, the questions are all *theory-driven*, i.e. existing theory (cf. the above model) is used as a basis for the questions raised. In fact, a prime value of theory is to identify factors (variables), relate them to each other and examine such relationships to provide explanations.

In the above examples, questions were used to 'structure' the problem. By using existing knowledge, the researcher will often be able to structure the problem so that, for example, hypotheses may be derived and tested.

Do I ask the important question(s)?

Problems may be more or less understood. A distinction is often made between 'structured' and 'unstructured' problems. It should be noted that it is not the problems *per se*, but the understanding of the problems that is more or less structured. The degree of structure of the research problem has implications for the choice of research design and research methods. Research practice is also influenced by the researcher's philosophy of science, perspective (cf. Chapter 2), training and so on. How understanding of the problem influences the choice of research design is dealt with in Chapter 4. The notions of quantitative and qualitative methods (see Chapter 8) relate partly to differences in problem structure, but also to differences in philosophy of science and perspective held by the researcher.

3.2 The research process

Research is often thought of as a *process*, i.e. a set of interrelated activities unfolding over time. The starting point in Figure 3.1 is the problem to be studied (1). The problem, whatever it might be and how it is perceived and defined, is the point of departure in research.

Any problem dealt with is *represented* in one way or another, i.e. the problem is represented by a 'model', either implicit or explicit (1a). (Models are dealt with in section 3.4.) The problem and how it is perceived influence:

- choice of research design;
- measurements;
- data collection;
- sample;

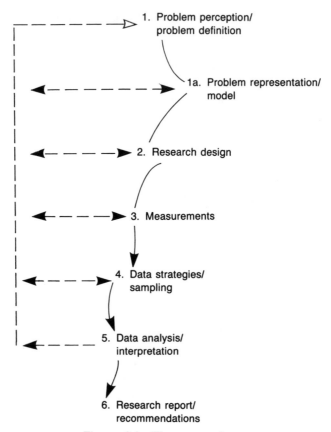

Figure 3.1   The research process

- data analysis; and
- recommendations.

Research design (2) relates to the choice of strategy to collect the information needed. The remaining part of Figure 3.1 relates to activities such as designing adequate measurements (operational definitions) (3) and strategies for collecting the data needed (4). The data collected must be processed, analyzed and interpreted (5). Finally, to be of any use the produced findings must be communicated and used (6).

Figure 3.1 may give the impression that research comprises structured, sequential activities. This is often not the case. For example, when working with the problem representation, the original problem may be reframed or, when working with the research design or analyzing the data, new insights may emerge that influence the understanding of the problem. Thus, research activities are often interrelated, as indicated by the broken feedback lines. The remaining part of this chapter relates to the first two steps in Figure 3.1, i.e. the conceptual foundations of doing research.

3.2.1 Conceptual (theoretical) and empirical level

In Figure 3.1, a distinction may be drawn between activities at steps 1 and 1a, which may be classified as activities at the *conceptual (theoretical) level*, and activities related to steps 2−5, which are at the *empirical* level. The following should be noted. *All* research — irrespective of discipline — requires activities at the conceptual level. So-called 'theoretical studies' are at this level only. For example, studies in mathematics and pure (theoretical) economics relate primarily to specific problems without seeking empirical evidence. Also, in business administration important contributions have been made that are primarily 'theoretical' (even though inspired by empirical observations), such as the influential contributions of J.D. Thompson (*Organizations in Action*) and J.G. March and H.A. Simon (*A Behavioral Theory of the Firm*), which have shaped much of the thinking and research in business administration disciplines.

NB Any empirical study — even studies for practical business purposes — requires efforts at the conceptual level. Bypassing such activities and jumping to the 'raw empirical data' is seldom, if ever, very successful. The fact that this is often done in business does not mean that such research is good; rather, it reflects a lack of insight.

Know your research problem!

3.2.2 Research and knowledge

Doing research also implies that we *add* to present knowledge, i.e. research is done to create new insights. For example, if a business firm conducts a study to examine what buyers emphasize, this is done to create new insights believed to be important to the firm. Knowledge can be classified in various ways (Naegel, 1961). For example:

- theories/models;
- concepts;
- methods/techniques; and
- facts.

New insights can be acquired in any of the above categories. The researcher may develop a new theory to describe and explain how buyers behave. New methods or techniques can be developed to assist business managers in their decision making, and new facts may be uncovered. For example, before entering a new market, the firm needs knowledge to assess the size of and the competitive situation in the market.

New insights may also be acquired by demonstrating new practical implications of a theory, by testing hypotheses derived from theory and by applying a method to a new problem. The important point is that any research should have an *intended contribution*, i.e. bring something new.

What is the intended contribution of my study?

3.2.3   *What comes first: theory or research?*

In the research literature, a distinction is often made between the following two strategies:

- theory before research; and
- research before theory.

In the first case, present knowledge allows for structuring the research problem so that the researcher knows what to look for, what factors are relevant and what hypotheses should be tested empirically. From the above discussion it follows that, when wrestling with problems, the researcher also makes (or at least should make) use of available knowledge.

Figure 3.2 illustrates the two research strategies. In the first case (1), important tasks are to identify relevant concepts, theories and so on, and to adjust the concepts (theory) to the problem under scrutiny (which also requires a clear understanding of the research problem). In the latter case, the prime task is to identify relevant factors and construct explanations (theory).[2]

It is also important to be aware that theories/methods and concepts are *general*, i.e. they allow for subsuming a variety of specific research problems, which of course is useful. On the other hand, when general, the various theories, concepts or models possess almost no content about the actual problem. The researcher's task is thus to give the concepts/theories/models content.

Example

The notion of the 'value chain' is known to any student who has had a course in business strategy. To become of any use for the firm, this general term must be adjusted to the

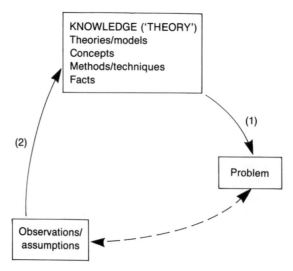

Figure 3.2   Production and use of theory

specific firm in question. This may include the identification and classification of the actual firm's activities as well as linkages between the activities. In order to make use of the general concepts (theories), the researcher must be able to *select*, *adjust* and *apply* such tools to her or his specific problem. This is a demanding task which requires insights and training. Misuse and non-use of relevant knowledge — as frequently observed — reflects the lack of such skills (and does not mean, as is often believed, that it is 'practical').

The second strategy (2), research before theory, starts with observations/gathering of data. A couple of things should, however, be noted before choosing such a strategy:

- There should be a *reason* for choosing such an approach. If relevant knowledge already exists, this easily ends up 'reinventing the wheel' (cf. the above discussion of understanding the research problem).
- This approach implies 'theory construction', which is different from 'theory testing' (cf. note 3). The knowledge/skill requirements for doing such research are different from those for doing structured theory testing, but are equally demanding and include the use of statistical methods. Most students in business administration have almost *no* training in such research. If for some reason the student dislikes, say, statistics, this in *no* way guarantees that s/he can do a good 'theory-constructing' study; rather, the opposite will be the case.

In Figure 3.2, there is also a broken line between the two strategies, indicating that when applying present insights to specific problems, new observations and new questions may give rise to a search for new explanations or new methods/techniques.

3.3   Concepts: building blocks in research

Concepts are the building blocks of any theory or model (see section 3.4). A concept is an abstraction representing an object, a property of an object or a certain phenomenon. 'Cost', 'income', 'market share' and 'business strategy' are all examples of common concepts in business administration disciplines.

Concepts are crucial in the researcher's 'toolbag'. They serve a number of important functions, such as the following:[3]

- Concepts are the foundation of *communication*. Without a set of agreed concepts, meaningful communication is impossible.
- Concepts introduce a *perspective*: a way of looking at the empirical world.
- Concepts are a means for *classification* and generalization.
- As noted above, concepts serve as components of theories (models) and thus of explanations and predictions.

Concepts are the most critical element in any theory (model) because they *guide what is captured*. For example, the concepts 'cognitive' and 'dissonance' direct the theory of cognitive dissonance, and 'supply' and 'demand' are key concepts in economic theory. Even though many concepts used in everyday life are ambiguous (such as 'democracy'

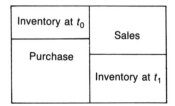

Figure 3.3   Operational definition of sales during a specific time interval

and 'influence'), they must be clear and agreed upon to be useful in research. Clarification and precision of concepts are achieved through *definitions*. Here we will distinguish between two types of definition, conceptual and operational.

Definitions that describe concepts by using other concepts are *conceptual definitions*. An example is the concept of 'market' as defined in the marketing literature, i.e. 'all the potential customers sharing a need or want who might be willing and able to engage in exchange to satisfy that need or want'. In this definition, 'customers' and 'need'/'want' are among the concepts used to define the concept of market (Kotler, 1991).

Another example is the concept of 'industry', defined in strategy literature as 'the group of firms producing products that are close substitutes for each other' (Porter, 1980). Here 'firms', 'products' and 'substitutes' are key concepts to explain industry.

To be useful, definitions should have the following properties:

● They should point out *unique* attributes or qualities of whatever is defined.
● They should *not be circular*, i.e. they must not contain any part of the thing being defined. Defining 'market exchange' as 'exchange taking place in the market' does not enhance communication.
● They should be stated *positively*, i.e. contain the properties of the concept defined.
● They should use *clear* terms.

> What concepts are used to map my research problem?
> Are the concepts properly defined?

An *operational definition* is a set of procedures that describes the activities required to establish empirically the existence or degree of existence of what is described by a concept. Operational definitions are crucial in measurement. They tell what to do and what to observe in order to bring the phenomenon defined within the range of the researcher's experience. For example, 'market share' may be defined operationally as: Company's sales of products in category X in area A during time t/Total sales of product category X in area A during time t, which also requires specifications of 'sales', product category X, area and time period.

In accounting, 'sales' during a specific time interval are often defined operationally as shown in Figure 3.3, or:

Sales = Inventory at t_0 + Purchase during the period $(t_0 - t_1)$ —
Inventory at t_1

This definition gives sales as measured in cost (purchase) prices or in terms of volume (quantity). (If measured in sales prices, profit will hopefully be present.)

Note that the observed market share may differ according to whether it is measured in volume or money (value), and if it is based on money, according to whether the cost or sales price is used to estimate 'sales'. Operational definitions will be dealt with in more detail when discussing measurements (see Chapter 5).

Theory may be viewed as a system for ordering concepts in a way that produces understanding or insights. A theory includes more than one concept and the concepts are linked together. One definition of theory is given below (Zaltman *et al.*, 1982: 71).

'A set of interrelated concepts, definitions and propositions that present a systematic view of specifying relations among variables with the purpose of explaining and predicting phenomena.'

It is important to note that the purpose of theory is to *explain*, which is related to understanding as well as *prediction*. For example, a researcher holds a theory of how 'advertising works' and uses this theory to allocate the firm's advertising budget based on a prediction of the outcome of the advertising money. Also note the idea of 'proposition', i.e. an assumed relationship between two concepts such as 'performance' and 'satisfaction'.

The above definition of theory also claims that it should present a systematic view to enhance explanation and prediction,[4] i.e. the concepts and relationships involved should represent a coherent 'whole'.

When we move from the conceptual to the empirical level in research, concepts are converted into *variables* by mapping them into a set of values. For example, assigning numbers to objects involves the mapping of a set of objects into a set of numbers. A variable is a property that takes two or more values (while a constant has one value only). For example:

Construct	Variable
height	... 150, ... 180 cm
sex	1 (= women), 0 (= men)

3.4 Models in research

In our above discussion, the research problems were — through questions — mapped by a limited set of factors (variables). When dealing with a research problem, some *representation* of the problem is present. This will also be the case in real life. For example, when a business manager instructs his employee to smile, the following representation or *model* may be in his head: 'When my employees smile, the customers feel comfortable and are more willing to buy.' The manager's model can be illustrated as follows:

$$\text{Smiling employees} \rightarrow \text{Customers feel well} \rightarrow \text{Willingness to buy}$$

We all hold such representations/models. Often, however, they are implicit and ambiguous.

In research, models play a predominant role. They are closely related to the notion of theory, as they imply a systematic organization of concept. Key characteristics of a model are as follows:

- *Representation*, i.e. the object or phenomenon is represented by the model. The model is not the object or phenomenon itself.
- *Simplification*: a model simplifies by reducing the number of variables included.
- *Relationship(s)* exist(s) between the variables included.

Example

Above we used the following model (often termed the 'model of profit planning') known to business students:

$$\text{Profit} = (\text{Price} - \text{Variable cost}) \cdot \text{Quantity} - \text{Fixed cost}$$

First, this model is a general representation to capture economic aspects important to firms (and is definitely not the firm itself). Second, it is definitely a simplification, as a variety of other factors that may influence the firm and its performance are left out. Note how *few* concepts (variables) are used, i.e. costs (variable and fixed), quantity, price and profit. Third, it is easily seen that the various factors are related. By changing, say, price and keeping the other factors to the right of the equals sign constant, profit will change.

In research (and this is also the case in practical research), a prime task is to 'structure' the problem. This to a substantial degree relates to identifying relevant factors and relating them to each other in order to *map* and *frame* the problem under scrutiny.

> What are the crucial concepts (variables) in my problem representation?

3.4.1 Model purposes

Models may be used for a variety of purposes. At the general level, we may distinguish between:

- description;
- explanation;

- prediction/forecasting; and
- guidance of activities.

1. A *description* tells us how 'things are'. An example of a descriptive model is the organizational chart. Figure 3.4 represents a (naive) description of the *formal* organization. Note that this general model contains only *one* class of variables, i.e. positions. The direction of the lines indicates authority — responsibility relationships. A has formal authority over B. B is responsible to A. B and C are at the same authority level.

Are such simple models useful in business research? Description of the formal authority in a firm may be combined with analysis and assessment of the knowledge and skill requirements of the various positions, and can thus be used for the identification of knowledge gaps to be filled. Descriptions of the actual formal structure may be compared to some 'ideal' structure, which may be used for improving the organizational structure; or such descriptions, conducted at different points in time, may be used to study structural changes.[5]

Descriptions come in many forms. Assume that a researcher wants to describe the *informal* organization of a company. This requires a specified and detailed definition of the concept 'informal organization', including *what aspects* should be addressed. For example, the researcher may end up studying the communication flow in the company, i.e. who is interacting with whom; or s/he may study who influences decisions to uncover potential deviations in communication flow or power from that reflected in the formal organizational chart. Another example is the researcher who wants to study the buying behaviour of a firm's business customers. Depending on its purpose, the study can be framed in several ways. The study may focus on *what* the business firms are buying, or on *how* the business firms buy. This may include mapping how buying processes are triggered off, events taking place and how they are related in the buying processes.

Making good descriptions requires skills.
What aspects to include depends on the purpose of the study!

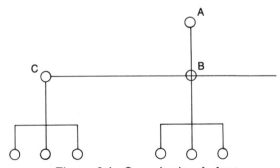

Figure 3.4 **Organizational chart**

2. Many studies are conducted to *explain* phenomena. The well-known model of 'profit planning' shown at the beginning of this section may be used for explanation purposes. In this model, profit is explained by the difference between unit price and variable cost per unit times quantity sold minus fixed costs.

A researcher wants to explain why some firms succeed while others fail in an industry. This requires a definition of what we mean by success. Moreover, it requires an identification of factors and processes that may produce success and failure.

Lave and March (1975) have proposed the following approach to map (model) problems:

(a) *Observe* some facts (e.g. success and/or failure of firms).
(b) Look at the facts as if they were the end results of some unknown *process* (model). Then speculate about the processes that might have produced such a result.
(c) Then *deduce* other results (implications/consequences/predictions) from the model.
(d) Then ask yourself whether these other implications are true and produce new models if necessary.

The major advices from the recommended approach are as follows:

● Think 'process'.
● Develop interesting implications.
● Look for generality.

When working with problems and models, it is important to keep it as *simple* as possible. More variables should only be included when it is useful, i.e. to improve the goodness of the explanation.

A good model — or, more correctly, its implications — should be *testable*. For example, the football team has just lost a game. The coach explains the loss as follows: 'I'm sorry. The problem was that our players didn't have enough fighting spirit, enough will to win.' The coach's (implicit) model can be depicted as follows:

Outcome (win/loss) = f (fighting spirit)

This model is *circular* as it explains any outcome. The model can never be falsified as it cannot be tested.

Can testable implications be derived from my model?

3. Many business studies are preoccupied with *prediction/forecasting*: forecasting of sales, prices and so on. In their simplest form, such predictions are based on extrapolation of past behaviour (development). For example, the following model has been developed to predict population size in a given area:

$$P_{t_i} = P_{t_0} \cdot 1.007^{(t_i - t_0)}$$

where:

P_{t_i} = population size at time t_i
P_{t_0} = population size at a specific point in time, e.g. 1 January 1995

Closer inspection of the model shows that it contains *one* variable only, i.e. time $(t_i - t_0)$. Both P_{t_0} and 1.007 are constants.

When calculating different values for $(t_i - t_0)$, 0, 1, 2, ..., n, a smoothly growing curve emerges. Is this a good or bad model? It only maps a specific pattern (depending on the size of the constants) and is unable to catch the impact of sudden changes, such as unemployment or people flocking to the area due to new business opportunities.

4. When models are used to *guide* business decisions, either a descriptive or an explanatory model must be complemented with a *rule of choice*. For example:

(a) Drop product if (Price − Variable cost) < Amount k.
(b) Drop product if (Price − Variable cost) · Quantity < Contribution c.
(c) After describing market size, enter market if total sales are greater than X.

3.5 Role of reviewing past literature

When business students are conducting a business study as part of their degree, they are supposed to use '*relevant* theory', i.e. demonstrate that they can apply *relevant* parts of the knowledge they are exposed to in the actual programme. There is nothing 'unpractical' in this, as most qualified research builds on prior knowledge (cf. Figure 3.2). To most business students, nagging questions are: 'What should I include?' and 'How should the literature be reviewed?'

In order to answer such questions, the following should be noted. Above we have emphasized the word 'relevant'. This means that what is included should be of *importance* for the study. Moreover, the following should be taken into account:

1. The prime *purposes* of the literature review are to:

(a) *frame* the problem under scrutiny;
(b) *identify* relevant concepts, methods/techniques and facts; and
(c) *position* the study (NB Any study should add something 'new').

Wrestling with a research problem involves searching for structure and the identification of the 'real' problem, i.e. trying to answer questions such as: 'What do I want to know?' and 'How do I want to map the problem?' (cf. the above discussion of problems and models). As noted above, such questions are important in research (cf. Figure 3.1). A useful strategy at the initial stage of the project is to expose oneself to a variety of sources dealing with the topic: for example, by reading journal articles and textbooks, and by discussing with 'experts', such as the professor and people from the industry.

Hint: To get quick insights, start with recent 'state-of-the-art reviews', which are available in most disciplines. An example from international marketing is Bradley (1987).

It should be noted that broad exposure to information and 'incubation' are considered important in most creative techniques. Then, after this exposure to information, start active questioning to frame the problem. The more precisely the problem can be stated, the better direction there is for the research activities to follow. This will also help clarify what the *intended contribution* of the study is supposed to be (cf. section 3.2).

2. Based on the above activities (1), the researcher should be able to state the *criteria* for what to include in the written literature review.

3. Based on (2), a *systematic* search should be made for relevant contributions — for example, using computerized library services — and the various sources gathered to supplement the initial search (1).

4. In writing up the literature review, conscious consideration should be given to what to emphasize. If the focus is on mapping the problem, the emphasis may be on prior conceptualizations. If, however, the main focus is on how the variables should be measured, the focus may be on measurement procedures used in prior studies. (This implies that literature inspected need not necessarily be included in the written literature review. What to include should be determined by the problem and the criteria used.)

5. A literature review should also include *evaluation* and *critique* of the literature reviewed. Based on such evaluation and critique, the researcher's own choice of conceptualization and research design should be argued for.

> The main purpose of the literature review is to structure the research problem and to position the study.

NB Search for and review of literature takes time, not least because it is demanding and time consuming to get hold of the research problem. Therefore, try to get a head start! Reading *and* thinking often produce fruitful results!

3.6 Concluding remarks

Research is often associated with constructing and designing questionnaires, measurements, statistical procedures and so on, which can be subsumed under the umbrella-concept 'research methodology'. Research methodology can be conceived as a system of rules and procedures. Such rules and procedures are important in research for several purposes:

- Research methodology can be conceived as rules for *reasoning*, i.e. a specific logic to acquire insights.
- Research methodology is important for *intersubjectivity*. Reporting (in detail) how the reseacher has obtained his or her findings means that they can be evaluated by others.
- Research methodology can also be considered as rules for *communication*. Reporting on the rules and procedures used enables others to try to replicate them, or they can criticize the approach chosen and the findings reported.

Qualifying research requires competence in logical reasoning and analysis. The researcher thus needs to have command over the research methodology to be used. Research methodology is thus an important tool in the researcher's toolbag. Research, however, is also closely related to finding, selecting, structuring and solving problems. In order to grasp, represent and understand problems, concepts, theories and models are crucial. Theoretical knowledge and the ability to think conceptually are important and a prerequisite for doing qualifying research. Problems represent the point of departure in research. Perception and the structuring of problems influence subsequent research activities.

Qualifying empirical research requires both conceptual and methodological insights. Skills related to topics dealt with in this chapter are crucial to making relevant use of other tools in research.

Notes

1. A key assumption is that researchers advance knowledge not by verifying, but by falsifying, i.e. by letting the assumed hypothesis be tested so that it can be rejected. Inspect any introductory textbook in statistics. A good description of hypothesis testing is also found in Churchill (1991).
2. This relates to different contexts of research, i.e. the 'context of justification' and 'context of discovery', respectively. See Popper (1961) for lucid discussion.
3. See Frankfort-Nachmias and Nachmias (1992) for a more complete discussion.
4. See Frankfort-Nachmias and Nachmias (1992) for a more complete discussion of functions and types of theory.
5. Comparisons of structural description(s) at different points in time (t), S_t, S_{t_1}, . . ., can be seen as a special case of comparative static analysis as frequently used in economics. Changes are inferred by comparing the static descriptions from different points in time.

CHAPTER 4

Research designs

The scientist is a man with a problem — or he is nothing.

(Scott Geer, 1969)

The research design is the overall plan for relating the conceptual research problem to relevant — and doable — empirical research. This chapter focuses on important problems to be handled by the researcher in selecting an adequate research design for her or his empirical study.

4.1 The design problem

Empirical research is conducted to answer research questions. Choice of *research design* is the overall strategic choice made with the purpose of coming up with an approach that allows for answering the research problem in the best possible way — within the given constraints. In other words, a research design should be *effective* in producing the wanted information within the *constraints* put on the researcher, such as time, budgetary and skill constraints. This last point is important, even though too frequently overlooked. In business, research results must often be produced within strict time constraints, limiting the number of possible research options. The business student also usually has a limited amount of time to produce a research report for her or his degree. In most cases, the amount of money available for doing the research is also limited and the student's research competence (usually) has its limitations as well.

Choice of research design can be conceived as the overall strategy to get the information wanted. This choice influences the subsequent research activities, such as what data to collect and how they should be collected. The renowned social scientists Kornhauser and Lazarsfeld (1955) once claimed that research designs played the role of 'master techniques', while statistical analysis of the data collected was termed 'servant techniques'.

Design errors occur too often. Such errors frequently occur by neglecting the design problem. The typical approach: 'Let's prepare a questionnaire and get some data' easily ends up with 'a bunch of data' which, after time is out and the money used, leaves the researcher (student) with 'a bunch of data searching for a problem'.

Other common mistakes are making wrong and/or irrelevant design choices, such as examining a badly understood problem with a very structured design or, even more common as 'qualitative methods' have become increasingly popular, examining structured, well-understood problems with 'unstructured' methods, making it difficult to answer the research problem adequately. The importance of the problem − research design relationship is discussed below.

> What do I really want to answer through my research?

4.2 Problem structure and research design

Research problems are infinite and they come in many forms. Consider the following examples:

- The political party wants to conduct a poll to examine its share of voters. This is a structured problem. The political party knows what information is wanted, i.e. the fraction (or percentage) of voters.
- An advertising company has produced two advertisement copies and wants to know which one is the more effective for use in advertising campaigns. Again, the research problem is structured. The advertising agency wants to know which (if either) of the two advertisement copies (A and B) is better, i.e. whether $A > B$, $B > A$ or $A = B$. Moreover, in this case advertisement is seen as a 'cause' which may produce some effect, such as awareness, interest or sales.
- Company X's sales have dropped for three consecutive months. The management does not know why. In this case, the management has made an observation, i.e. dropping sales. The management does not know what has caused the decline in sales. This is a more unstructured problem.

The above examples show (among other things) that problems may vary in structure, i.e. how well they are understood. Based on problem structure, we may distinguish between the three main classes of research design:

	Research design	*Problem structure*
1.	Exploratory	Unstructured
2.	Descriptive	Structured
3.	Causal	Structured

1. When the research problem is badly understood, a (more or less) *exploratory* research design is adequate. An example will illustrate this. Consider your favourite Friday night detective series. Most such stories start with a phone call leading the detective hero to a dead person, apparently murdered. The problem the detective is confronted with is: 'Who did it: who is guilty (if anyone)?' How does the detective proceed? He or she collects data and tries to find some lead thread. As new information emerges, the picture becomes clearer and at the end the detective finds the answer.

A key characteristic when examining the detective's approach to solving the problem is its *flexibility*. As new pieces of information are made available, the search for a solution may change direction. But there is more to this.

(a) Research problems may be more or less understood. There is *no* reason not to use available *a priori* information. Like the detective, the researcher may have 'suspects'. This is often the case in medical research, where potential causes are examined in a laboratory experimental setting. (This indicates that even experiments (see section 4.4) can be used in exploratory research.)
(b) As with other types of research, exploratory research should be conducted in the best possible way.
(c) Exploratory research, like other types of research, requires skills, but the skill requirements differ. Key skill requirements in exploratory research are an ability to observe, get information and construct explanation (i.e. theorizing).

2. In *descriptive* research, the problem is structured and well understood. Consider the case where the firm wants to examine the 'size of market M'. The problem as such, i.e. the task to solve, is clear. What is needed is, first, a classification of what is meant by 'market'. Is it the number of people, actual and potential buyers of a specific product group within a specific area within a specified time period, or . . .? (Cf. the above discussion of concepts and definitions.) Assume agreement on the latter interpretation, i.e. actual and potential buyers of a specific product group (e.g. X) within a specified time period (e.g. one year). The researcher's task is now to produce this information. What would be the best research strategy?

Assume that relevant secondary data are not available. The researcher plans to collect the data by a survey study using personal interviews. A detailed sampling plan must be made with regard to how many people and whom to interview. The research must also construct questions, i.e. measurements to get information about the purchase (or use) of the product. (To make good measurements is crucial in research: see Chapter 5 for detailed discussion.) Then procedures must be established for how the interviews shall be conducted, questions reported and so on. All interviews should be conducted in the same way so that the variation in the data collection is as small as possible. Thus, key characteristics of descriptive research are *structure* and *precise rules and procedures*. A good example is the procedure used by medical doctors when examining a person's height. The person has to take his shoes off, stretch his leg, look straight ahead. The same procedure is used for *all* persons measured.

Descriptive studies may include more than one variable. For example, suppose the research wants to describe smokers by social class. Again, the researcher is confronted

Table 4.1 Cross-table

		Social class				
		I	II	III	IV	Total
Smoke	Yes					
	No					
	Total	100%	100%	100%	100%	100%
	$n =$	( )	( )	( )	( )	( )

with conceptual and definitional problems. When these are solved, procedures for collecting the data must be determined to produce the data needed for answering the research question. In this case, the task can be conceived of as completing the cross-table shown in Table 4.1.

3. In *causal* research, the problems under scrutiny are structured as well. However, in contrast to descriptive research, in this case the researcher is also confronted with 'cause-and-effect' problems, as illustrated in the advertising example above. The main tasks in such research are to isolate cause(s), and to tell whether and to what extent 'cause(s)' result(s) in effect(s). Examples of questions in causal research are: 'Is the medical drug effective?' and 'What dose is the most effective?' In the following sections, such problems are discussed more fully.

What type of research design is appropriate for my research problem?

4.3 The problem of 'cause'

The problem of 'cause' and 'effect' is an old one and has intrigued scientists for hundreds of years. It is beyond the scope of this book to review various perspectives on this problem.[1] The main objective is to focus on some key characteristics of the problem.

Consider the following examples:

- A dealer has reduced the price on TV sets by 10 per cent and the sales have increased by 20 per cent. Is the price reduction a (the) cause of the increased sales?
- Managers are often preoccupied with 'success factors'. For example, in the well-known book *In Search of Excellence*, Peters and Waterman (1982) claim that 'being close to the customers' is an important factor in explaining success. Is closeness to customers a cause of success?

Table 4.2 Covariation

		Price reduction				Close to customers	
		Yes (10%)	No			Yes	No
Sales increase	Yes	20%	—	Success	Yes	30%	—
	No	80%	100%		No	70%	100%
		100%	100%		Σ	100%	100%

1. In order to be a cause, *concomitant variation* is needed, i.e. there should be a covariation between the cause and the effect. For example, there should be covariation between price reduction and change in sales. Examples of such covariations are shown in Table 4.2.

   In both the above examples, 'effect' (i.e. sales increase and success, respectively) is present only when 'cause' is present (i.e. price reduction and closeness to customers). Inspection of Table 4.2 also shows that 'effect' is not always present when cause is present. For example, in 80 per cent of cases with price reductions, no increase in sales occurs. This indicates that *if* price reduction can be considered a cause, the cause – effect relationship is, at best, *probabilistic*, i.e. it is more likely that sales will increase when price reductions are present than when this is not the case.
2. The cause should *precede* the effect. Did the price change take place before the sales increase? If closeness to customers is a cause, this should be established before the firm's success. Thus, the *time order* of occurrence of variables is important.
3. Other possible causal factors should be eliminated. Did the sales increase occur immediately after the announcement of the reduction in the price of TV sets? Or was the sales increase observed the week before a big sporting event, such as the Olympics? Thus, a key requirement is to *rule out alternative* causes. For example, can the firm's success be explained by superior products, cost control or market power?

   The problem of ruling out other factors is also present even when one is not confronted with causal problems. Researchers often observe covariation: for example, as measured by the correlation coefficient.[2] An important question is whether an observed correlation coefficient (e.g. between advertising spent and sales) is a 'true' one, or whether the covariation changes or disappears when controlling for other factors, such as size of market or type of product.

4.3.1 The importance of theory

The question of cause and effect also calls for *a priori* theory in research. The need for theory can be illustrated in the following way. Assume two variables, X and Y. For these two variables, the following relationships are possible:

1. $X \rightarrow Y$ (X causes Y)
2. $Y \rightarrow X$ (Y causes X)
3. $X \rightleftharpoons Y$ (mutual causation)
4. $X \neq Y$ (no relationship)

For two variables there are thus four possible relationships. Assume a study involving six variables. With six variables there are $\binom{6}{2} = 15$ two-variable combinations, which amount to $4^{15} > 1073$ million potential relationships. Without *a priori* theory, i.e. knowledge of what to look for, it will be almost impossible to muddle through.

4.4 The classical experiment

Possible research designs are multiple. Below is reported the classical experiment in its simplest form. Even though many (most) business studies are not experimental, the classical experimental research design is useful for understanding all other designs.

In Figure 4.1, O_1 etc. denote observations. X is the experimental stimulus. Observations are made both before (pre-test) and after (post-test) manipulation of the experimental stimulus. Two groups are included: the experimental group, i.e. the group which the experimental stimulus is assigned to; and a control group not exposed to the experimental stimulus. R indicates randomization, i.e. the subjects are randomly assigned to the two groups.

	Experimental group	Control group
	R	R
Pre-test	O_1	O_3
	X	
Post-test	O_2	O_4
Difference	$(O_2 - O_1)$	$(O_4 - O_3)$

Figure 4.1 The classical experiment

The *independent* variable is the experimental stimulus. In the present case, the experimental variable (the 'treatment') takes two values only, i.e. the experimental stimulus, can be present (1) and absent (0) respectively. The dependent variable is some effect measure. If the experimental stimulus has an effect, then $(O_2 - O_1) > (O_4 - O_3)$.

In the experiment, the researcher has control over the independent variable(s), i.e. the research can *manipulate* the various experimental conditions. As will be discussed below, outside factors may also influence the observed effect. The impact of outside influences is assumed 'levelled out' through randomization.

Table 4.3 Reported improvement in the test and control groups

		Group		
		Test	Control	Total
Feel better	Yes	80%	20%	50%
	No	20%	80%	100%
	Total	100%	100%	100%
	$n =$	(50)	(50)	(100)

Why use control groups? If a group was given some treatment, such as a medical drug for a headache, it is impossible to evaluate whether the drug had any effect at all, as most people recover from headaches without taking medical drugs at all.

Examples

Assume 100 people with diagnosed influenza were randomly assigned to two groups: a test group, which was given an effective drug, and a control group, which was given an ineffective drug (a placebo).[3] The subjects were instructed to come back in one week, and then asked: 'Do you feel better?'

Inspection of Table 4.3 shows that a higher fraction of the test group reports 'better' than is the case for the control group. The difference in reported improvement is statistically significant ($p < 0.001$), i.e. it is very likely that the drug has had an effect. The treatment is considered a 'cause' in the present case. Because of control, i.e. the ability to manipulate the treatment and randomization, one may be rather confident that the effective medical drug really can be seen as a cause for improvement.

Figure 4.1 and Table 4.3 show the experiment in its most simple form. The independent variable (the treatment) can definitely take more than two values. For example, assume that a company is interested to know which one of the following selling strategies is the most effective: S_1 (phone call), S_2 (advertisement), S_3 (personal selling) or S_4 (personal selling + advertising).

More than one independent variable (treatment) may also be included. Assume one variable (treatment), selling a message using either (1) one-sided or (2) two-sided arguments, and another variable, gender, i.e. whether the salesperson is (1) a woman, or (2) a man. In this case it is possible to capture the effects of:

● type of message;
● gender; and
● interaction effect (if any).

Assume that an experiment has been conducted and the results in Table 4.4 observed. When looking at part (a) of Table 4.4, it is seen that the effectiveness score (e.g. sales) is the highest for two-sided messages, both for women $(60 - 50) = 10$ and for men $(50 - 40) = 10$. It is also seen that the reported effects are larger for women, both for one-sided

Table 4.4 The effects of message and gender

		(a) Message			(b) Message	
		One-sided	Two-sided		One-sided	Two-sided
Gender	Women	50	60	Women	50	70
	Men	40	50	Men	40	50

$(50 - 40) = 10$ and two-sided $(60 - 50) = 10$ messages. It is also seen that the differences between one- and two-sided messages are the same for both women and men. This indicates that *no* interaction effect is present.

Moving on to part (b) of Table 4.4, it is seen that the difference between two- and one-sided messages is higher for women $(70 - 50) = 20$ than for men $(50 - 40) = 10$. This indicates that an interaction effect between gender and message is present.

> Do I want to 'explain' something?
>
> Do I know my independent and dependent variables?
>
> Is an experiment appropriate?

4.5 Validity threats

A key purpose of the experimental design is to isolate and estimate the effect(s) of potential cause(s) (cf. section 4.3). The experiment is a 'powerful' design as it allows for the manipulation of treatment (cause) before and after measurements, and thus for the identification of covariation between treatment (cause) and effect, of time order (cause precedes effect) and of the effect of other explanations (randomization). The idea of experimental design is useful in many studies. Some examples are the pre-test of alternative advertisement copies, studying the effectiveness of various selling strategies, and field tests of marketing programmes.

The researcher wants to obtain *valid* knowledge (cf. section 3.2), i.e. s/he wants results that are 'true'. For example, if a study shows that advertisement A is more effective than advertisement B, the researcher should be confident that this is the case. There are many types of validity.[4] In the above advertisement case, the question of validity refers to *internal* validity, i.e. the question of whether the results obtained *within* the study are true. *External* validity, on the other hand, refers to the question of whether the findings can be *generalized*: for example, to other populations, settings or periods.

There are several *threats* to validity, for example the following four:

1. *History*, i.e. specific events external to the study (experiment) that occur at the same time and that may affect the response (criterion variable). For example, consider the TV store reducing the prices by 10 per cent and observing a sales increase of 20 per cent. A potential external threat is the announcement of a price increase for TV sets next month. Note that the experiment (cf. Figure 4.1), by including one (or more) control group(s), allows for controlling for the impact of such effects.

2. *Maturation*, i.e. processes operating within the test units in the study as a function of the passage of time *per se*. For example, a patient has received a medical drug and recovers. Patients often recover without such treatment. Thus, what is the cause of the patient's recovery, the medical drug or her or his immune system? Maturation is a serious threat to validity in many studies.

To take another example, an organization recognizes the need for reorganization to enhance its performance and to survive, and succeeds in doing so. Is the success due to the reorganization *per se*, or could it be that the reorganization has made the employees aware of the serious situation and motivated them to perform better in order to keep their jobs? Notice that the experiment (in principle) allows for controlling for maturation effects.

3. *Test effect* indicates that the experiment/test itself may affect the observed response. For example, a group of employees is chosen for a specific programme and obtains superior results after the programme period. Is their performance caused by the programme or the fact that they are the chosen ones and thus motivated to perform?[5]

4. *Selection bias* (self-selection) is a serious threat to validity when the subjects are not (or cannot be) assigned randomly. For example, in assessing advertisement effects, the following procedure has frequently been applied (Colley, 1961). Assume the producer of the cigarette 'Z' wants to know whether an advertising campaign has been effective. A random sample of persons are asked the following questions:

Q1. 'Have you seen any advertisements for cigarettes during . . .?'
    'For what cigarettes?'
Q2. 'Have you bought cigarettes during . . .?' If yes, 'What brands?'

The results shown in Table 4.5 are obtained. It has been argued as follows: 20 per cent of those who have seen the advertisement bought, while only 5 per cent of those who did not see the advertisement bought. Thus the advertisement has 'contributed' with (20 − 5) per cent = 15 per cent.

Table 4.5 Reading of advertisement and purchase

		Seen advertisement for 'Z'		
		Yes	No	Total
Bought 'Z'	Yes	20	5	25
	No	80	95	175
	Total	100	100	200

Is the observed finding valid? It may be so, but the result may equally well be explained by other factors such as selective perception, i.e. persons who smoke and regularly buy the brand 'Z' are more inclined to see the advertisement for that brand.

What are the threats to validity in my study?
Are the threats to validity considered — and handled adequately?

4.6 Other research designs

In real life, it is often difficult (or impossible) to conduct a true experiment. For example, randomization may become impossible or it may be impossible to manipulate treatment. Experiments are most appropriate when studying *stimulus—response* relationships, i.e. in the situation where the 'treatment' can be manipulated or varies in a natural setting (natural experiments). Often the researcher is preoccupied with studying the relationships between *properties* and corresponding *dispositions*. For example, a researcher wants to study relationships such as organizational size and innovativeness, or gender (sex) and career paths. Intuitively, the researcher cannot manipulate the size of the organization or gender (sex). Moreover, when studying property—disposition relationships, the following difficulties may be encountered:

- The *time interval* can be rather long, often covering years or decades and making an experiment impossible. The relationship between gender (sex) and career is an example.
- The effects of properties are often *general*, lacking the specificity of the experimental stimulus, and thus make it difficult to establish the relationship between cause and effect.
- Establishment of identical groups to compare through randomization may also be difficult (or impossible).
- The time order of events is often difficult to determine when studying property—disposition relationships. For example, acquired properties like education can both determine and be determined by other factors.

Thus, the research design applied often deviates from the 'true' experiment. This, however, does not mean that the logic underlying the experiment is useless. In fact, the ideas underlying the experiment to make (valid) causal inferences can be applied to evaluate — and improve — the research even when the experimental design cannot be directly applied.

4.6.1 Cross-sectional designs

The study reported in Table 4.5 deviates from the classical experiment in several ways. There is no control group and there is no randomization. The 'cause' (advertisement

Table 4.6 Innovativeness by organizational size

		Organizational size		
		Small	Large	Total
Innovativeness	High	20%	80%	50%
	Low	80%	20%	100%
	Total	100%	100%	100%
	n =	(50)	(50)	(100)

Table 4.7 Control for 'third' variable

		Industry				
		I(1) Org. size		I(2) Org. size		
		Small	Large	Small	Large	Total
Innovativeness	High	80%	80%	20%	20%	50%
	Low	20%	20%	80%	80%	100%
	Total	100%	100%	100%	100%	100%
	n =	(25)	(25)	(25)	(25)	(100)

reading) and effect (purchase) variables are also measured at the *same time*. This is what
is termed a *cross-sectional* or *correlational* research design.

When looking more closely at Table 4.5, the researcher is confronted with several tasks
in order to 'prove' that advertising may 'cause' purchase. First, s/he must control for the
potential effect of other factors. What is termed 'control-for-third-variable' (which in fact
may also involve control for fourth, fifth (etc.) variables) exactly pinpoints this problem.
This can be done in several ways. Examine the cross-table between organizational size
and innovativeness shown in Table 4.6.

Inspection of Table 4.6 reveals that the innovativeness is apparently substantially
higher among large than among small organizations. The researcher wonders whether
'industry' may be an explanatory factor. In the present case, the sample of organizations
(firms) is from two industries, I(1) and I(2). By controlling for industry, the result shown
in Table 4.7 emerges.

Inspection of Table 4.7 now shows that organizational size has *no* effect. The variation
in innovativeness is explained by industry. Note that Table 4.7 is a simple, illustrative

example only. More than two categories of each variable can be included, as can control for more than one variable. The control for other variables can be done in several ways. In a correlation analysis, control can be done by using *partial* correlation analysis.[6]

To be a cause, the change in the causal factor should precede the effect. In cross-sectional research, data on independent and dependent variables are gathered at the same point in time (cf. Table 4.5). Often the researcher has some *a priori* knowledge to assume the time order of variables. For example, it may seem reasonable to assume that gender (sex) precedes choice of occupation. *A priori* knowledge is often used to establish 'weak' causal ordering, as is done in so-called path analysis and causal modelling (by use of LISREL).[7]

4.6.2   Time series

The researcher often acquires observations of a given phenomenon over time. A typical time design can be depicted as follows:

$$O_1 \; O_2 \; O_3 \; x \; O_4 \; O_5 \; O_6 \ldots$$

The problem confronted is to determine whether the independent variable (x) has had any effect. To what extent this is possible will partly depend on the problem, the number of observations and the observed pattern.

Example
President Kennedy's assassination occurred on 22 November 1963, and the Dow Jones Index of Industrial Stock Prices fell 21 points on that day. Is the assassination a potential cause of the decline in the Dow Jones Index? If variations of 21 points (or more) are common, it does not seem very likely. If, however, the index had been steadily increasing for some time and it was registered that the index value fell immediately after the announcement was known (as well as controlled that no other factors could explain the decline), it can be concluded that the assassination may be a possible cause of the decline in the Dow Jones Index, but examination of other potential causes of the index decline should be done before arriving at the final conclusion.

4.6.3   The one-shot case study

This design consists of observing a single group or event at a single point in time, usually after some phenomenon that may have produced change. Such a design may be depicted as part (a) of Figure 4.2.

In its pure form, the one-shot case study (part (a)) is an extremely weak design as it does not allow for any *comparisons*,[8] either with before the treatment (X) or with other, unexposed groups. The design can be improved by trying to 'reconstruct' the past, i.e. before X occurred, and by trying to make comparisons with some unexposed units during the period, indicated by broken arrows in part (b) of Figure 4.2.

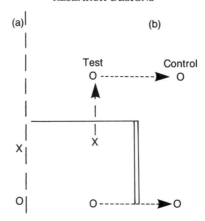

Figure 4.2   The one-shot case study

Usually case studies include multiple observations to be analysed. In other words, the 'case' may be more the *unit of observation* than the *unit of analysis*. For example, a researcher studies one firm intensively, with the purpose of getting insights into how decisions are made. S/he maps several decisions in detail, which are analyzed. Here each decision may be considered as a case. If well-planned, the case study secures *variations* along the variable included, allowing for comparisons of critical factors (see Campbell, 1975).

> What is the appropriate research design for my study?

4.7   Requirements in research design

When moving from the research problem at the conceptual level to empirical research, questions like 'How shall I proceed?' and 'How shall I do it?' arise. As noted at the outset of this chapter, the research design represents the overall strategy to gather the information needed to answer the research problem under scrutiny.

After thinking through what the research problem is, and how it should be represented (if possible: see section 4.2) and potential hypotheses (if any) derived, the first question to answer is: what *requirements* should the actual research design satisfy? A few examples will illustrate this point.

Examples

1. A study was conducted to explore whether firms (managers) within the same industry may perceive and interpret their surrounding environments differently and, if so, whether this might influence organizational actions and performance (Grønhaug and

Haukedal, 1989). A case study was chosen for research purposes. The following criteria were, however, established for the selection of the cases, i.e. firms should:

(a) belong to the same industry and be embedded in similar environments;
(b) be of approximately the same size;
(c) be in an industry where it is possible to identify major environmental change(s);
(d) at the outset have approximately the same economic resources; and
(e) have demonstrated different response(s) to the environmental change(s).

The above requirements also demonstrate that, even in 'qualitative' (case) research, *a priori* theorizing is (can be) useful to structure the research problem (cf. Chapter 3).

   2. Assume a study involving the following hypothesis:

H_1: The higher is the consumer's knowledge about her/his rights, the more likely s/he will be to complain.

Inspection of the above hypothesis shows that two constructs (variables) are included: (1) knowledge about rights, and (2) propensity to complain. The first requirement to test this hypothesis is information on these two variables. Moreover, *variations* in knowledge and propensity are needed. Reading of the hypothesis also shows that nothing is said about causation; only covariation between the two constructs (variables) is indicated. Thus, a cross-sectional (correlational) design is appropriate.

   3. Consider the following hypothesis:

H_2: An increase in advertising expenditure will increase the probability of getting orders.

Again, two variables are present: (1) advertising expenditure and (2) probability of getting orders. Information on these two variables is needed. The hypothesis also expresses a causal relationship, i.e. 'will increase'. In order to demonstrate causality, a design taking the time order between change (increase) in advertising expenditure and change in probability of getting orders is needed.

4.7.1   Research and choices

Research involves *choices* — problematic choices (see McGrath, 1982). When the design requirements have been specified, decisions must be made about how the requirements should be met and how the information needed should be collected. Important decisions include the following:

● How should the concepts (variables) be measured (operationalized)?
● What type of data? Secondary or primary?
● If secondary, what secondary data sources?
● If primary, how should the data be gathered? Through observation or interviewing?
● If interviewing, personal interviews by phone or through questionnaires?
● If interviewing, how should the questions be formulated? Structured or unstructured?

● Who should be interviewed? How should they be selected (sampling plan)? How many should be included (sample size)?

This list of questions is in no way complete, but clearly research involves choices. Quality research implies conscious, reasonable choices and the necessary skills in performing the activities involved.

Notes

1. For an excellent overview, see Cook and Campbell (1979), chapter 2.
2. A (Pearson) correlation (r) is a measure of covariation between two variables, X and Y, which can vary between -1 and $+1$. A correlation coefficient $r_{XY} = 1$ shows that the two variables covary perfectly.
3. This is done because giving a 'treatment' *per se* may have an effect on the subjects.
4. See Chapter 5 for a more detailed discussion, and Cook and Campbell (1979) for thorough treatment.
5. Test effects have been found to be a serious threat to validity, as in the 'Hawthorn studies', aiming to explain the impact of various work conditions.
6. The formula for the partial correlation coefficient $r_{12 \cdot 3}$ (read the partial correlation between (variable) 1 and 2 'dot' 3) is:

$$r_{12 \cdot 3} = \frac{r_{12} - (r_{13})(r_{23})}{\sqrt{1 - r_{13}^2} \, \sqrt{1 - r_{23}^2}}$$

The formula is iterative and thus, after controlling for variable 3, subsequent variables can be controlled for.
7. LISREL (linear structural equations) are now widely used. For an intuitive explanation, see Hair (1992), chapter 10.
8. This is an important point as all research involves some sort of *comparison*: for example, before and after; exposed and non-exposed; observed and expected.

CHAPTER 5

Measurements: mapping the empirical world

The GIGO principle: Garbage in — garbage out.

Business is 'context bound': it is related to specific markets, customer groups and competitive situations. Often the prime purpose of business studies is to gather information on this context in order to improve business decisions. For example, the firm may want to know the size of a given market, useful ways to segment the market, who the most likely purchasers are, and what they emphasize. Or the firm may want to know how decisions are made by industrial firms and who is involved. The purpose of business studies may also be more general, such as to examine the effectiveness of various advertising media. Problems that can be studied in business research are almost endless. Often studies are empirical, implying the gathering and use of data (to be dealt with in the chapters to follow).

Empirical research most often implies *measurements*. The reason for gathering data is to obtain information of importance for the research problem under scrutiny. The quality of the information depends considerably on the measurement procedures used in the gathering of data. In this chapter the concept of measurement is explained, levels (or scales) of measurement are discussed, and the importance of validity and reliability is emphasized. The chapter also offers advice for improving the quality of measurements in business research.

5.1 Defining measurement

We all make use of 'measurements' in everyday life, even though our measurements are often implicit or not considered as measurements at all. For example, a beauty contest can be conceived as some sort of measurement, as can picking the best advertisement or assessing the strength of the competitors. These examples all involve the *mapping* of some properties, which is a key element in all types of measurement. For example,

41

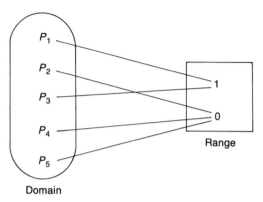

Figure 5.1   Mapping (assignment)

selected advertisements may be evaluated according to the use of colour, contents and so on, and through the use of some (usually implicit) rule a 'score' is obtained. Based on the 'scores', a rank order of the advertisements is established and the best one is chosen. A common observation, however, is that people often disagree on such judgements.

Why do people often disagree on everyday judgements?

Measurement can be defined as *rules for assigning numbers (or other numerals) to empirical properties*. A *numeral* is a symbol of the form I, II, III, . . ., or 1, 2, 3, . . . and has no quantitative meaning unless one gives it such a meaning. Numerals that are given quantitative meaning become numbers, which enable the use of mathematical and statistical techniques for descriptive, explanatory and predictive purposes. Thus, numbers are amenable to quantitative analyses, which may reveal new information about the items studied.

In the above definition, the term *assignment* means mapping. Numbers (or numerals) are mapped on to objects or events. Figure 5.1 illustrates the idea of mapping.

Figure 5.1 is read as follows. The domain is what is being mapped or measured. In the present case (Figure 5.1), the domain consists of five persons, P_1, . . ., P_5. Based on the characteristic, sex, they are mapped into 1 (= women) and 0 (= men) respectively.

The third concept used to define measurement is that of *rules*. A rule specifies the procedure according to which numbers (or numerals) are to be assigned to objects. Rules are the most significant component of the measurement procedure because they determine the quality of measurement. Poor rules make measurement meaningless. The function of rules is to tie the measurement procedure to some aspect of the 'reality'. Meaningful measurement is achieved only when it has an empirical correspondence with what is intended to be measured. Assume that we are going to measure some aspect of 'reality': for example, competitiveness, organizational climate or consumer satisfaction. The task ahead can be illustrated in the following way (see Figure 5.2).

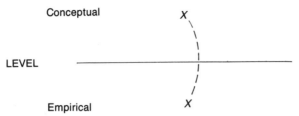

Figure 5.2 Measurement: the link between the conceptual and empirical levels

First, we need a good *conceptual definition* of the aspect to be measured, X (which in our case might be organizational competitiveness, market share and so on). Next, we need a *rule specifying* how to assign numbers to specific empirical properties. Thus, through measurements we can map some aspect of the empirical world. From this it is also seen that measurement is closely tied to the idea of operational definitions discussed previously (section 3.3 gave a few examples of operational definitions). Rules (operational definitions) are followed to obtain measurements.

So, why do people often disagree in their judgements? There might be several reasons. First, it has often not been clarified what aspects should be emphasized, i.e. clear conceptual definitions are lacking (cf. section 3.3). Next, the rules according to which scores are assigned are often implicit and the rules followed may even vary across observers.

5.1.1 Objects, properties and indicators

From the above discussion, it also follows that we are not measuring objects or phenomena as such. Rather, we measure specific properties of the objects or phenomena. For example, when studying human beings, a medical doctor might be interested in measuring properties such as height, weight or blood pressure. A cognitive psychologist might be interested in properties such as cognitive style and creativity, while a marketer

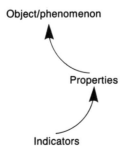

Figure 5.3 Object/phenomenon, properties and indicators

might focus on preferences and propensity to purchase among consumers in a specific market. To map such properties we use *indicators*, i.e. the scores obtained by using our operational definitions, such as responses to a questionnaire (see Figure 5.3).

> What do you think are relevant indicators to capture the concept of 'quality' for hotels?

5.2 Levels of measurement

In empirical research there is often a distinction between different levels of measurement (also termed 'scales of measurement'). This relates to specific properties of the obtained measurements, which determine the permissible mathematical and statistical operations (see Table 5.1).

5.2.1 Nominal level

The lowest level of measurement is the *nominal* level. At this level, numbers (or other symbols) are used to *classify* objects or observations. Objects that are alike are assigned

Table 5.1 Scales of measurement

Empirical scale averages	Basic operations	Measures of typical use	
Nominal	Determination of equality	Classification: Male–Female Occupations Social class	Median
Ordinal	Determination of greater or less	Rankings: Preference data Attitude measures	Median
Interval	Determination of equality of intervals	Index numbers: Temperature scales	Mean
Ratio	Determination of equality of ratios	Sales Units produced Number of customers	Mean

the same number (or symbol). For example, by means of the symbols 1 and 0, it is possible to classify a population into females and males, with 1 representing females and 0 males, respectively. The same population can be classified according to religion, place of living and so on. For example, the population in a city can be classified according to where they live: 1 = downtown, 2 = south, 3 = north, 4 = east, 5 = west.

5.2.2 Ordinal level

Many variables studied in business research are not only classifiable, they also exhibit some kind of relation, allowing for rank order. For example, we know that the grade A is better than the grade B, and B is better than C. We do not know the exact distance between A and B, and B and C, but we know that A > B > C ('>' greater, better than) or C < B < A ('<' less than). (When objects/persons can be ranked, they can of course also be ranked as equal: for example, B = B.)

5.2.3 Interval level

When we know the exact distance between each of the observations and this distance is constant, then an *interval* level of measurement has been achieved. This means that the differences can be compared. The difference between '1' and '2' is equal to the difference between '2' and '3'. The temperature scale is a classic example of an interval scale. But is 20°C twice as warm as 10°C? The answer is *no*. An example can demonstrate why this is so. John is 180 cm and Ann is 165 cm tall. The difference is 15 cm. Let us assume that we cut the scale so that 150 cm = 0. On this new scale, John is (180 − 150) = 30 and Ann is (165 − 150) = 15. Obviously, John is not 30/15 = 2, i.e. twice as tall as Ann. The reason is that the scale no longer has a natural zero.

NB By changing the scales, it is very easy to be misled.[1]

5.2.4 Ratio scale

The ratio scale differs from an interval scale in that it possesses a natural or absolute zero for which there is universal agreement as to its location. Height and weight are obvious examples. With a ratio scale, the comparison of absolute magnitude of numbers is legitimate. Thus, a person weighing 200 pounds is said to be twice as heavy as one weighing 100 pounds.

NB The more powerful scales *include* the properties possessed by the less powerful ones. This means that with a ratio scale we can compare intervals, rank objects according to magnitude, or use numbers to identify the objects.

The properties of measurement scales have implications for the choice of statistical techniques to be used in the analysis of the data. This will be dealt with in Chapter 9.

5.3   Validity and reliability in measurement

When we measure something, we want *valid* measures, i.e. measures capturing what they are supposed to. However, measurements often contain *errors*. The *observed* measurement score may (more or less) reflect the *true* score, but it may reflect other factors as well.[2] For example:

- *Stable characteristics*. It is known that people vary in *response set*, i.e. the way they respond. For example, some people tend to use the extreme ends of response scales, while others tend to centre their answers around the midpoints. Thus, two respondents, A and B, holding the same opinion, that a given product is good, may answer by circling their response alternatives on a seven-point scale as shown in Figure 5.4.
- The response may also be influenced by transient personal factors such as mood.
- Other factors that may influence the responses are situational factors, time pressure, variations in administration of the measurement and mechanical factors like checkmarks in the wrong box or incorrectly coded responses.

Figure 5.4   Seven-point scale

In order to clarify the notions of validity and reliability in measurement, we introduce the following equation:

$$X_O = X_T + X_S + X_R$$

where:

X_O = observed score
X_T = true score
X_S = systematic bias
X_R = random error

If the observed score equals the true score, i.e. $X_O = X_T$, the measurement is said to be perfectly *valid*.

Reliability refers to the stability of the measure. Let us assume that John's true height is 180 cm. The scale used, however, has been cut and repetitive measurements show that John is 170 cm. This, for one, indicates that the measure is reliable but not valid, i.e. the observed score, $X_O = X_T + X_S$. This tells us that a valid measure is also reliable. But a reliable measure does not need to be valid. Let us assume that John is measured by using a rubber-band. The obtained scores vary between 140 cm and 180 cm, with the mean

180 cm, which is his true height. In this case the random component, X_R, is height, and the measure is neither valid nor reliable.

In business studies we are often interested in studying relationships between variables. An example may illustrate how random measurement errors may influence the findings (see Figure 5.5).

In the present case the true, unobserved correlation coefficient between the two variables X (organizational climate) and Y (profitability) is $r = 0.8$. The correlation coefficients between the concept and obtained measure for the two variables are, however, in both cases $r = 0.5$. The *observed* relationship (correlation) is thus: $r_{X'.Y'} = r_{X'X} \cdot r_{XY} \cdot r_{Y'Y} = 0.8 \cdot 0.5 \cdot 0.5 = 0.2$, which is considerably lower than the true relationship. (This simple example assumes that the observed $r_{X'Y} = 0.2$ is influenced by factors reported in Figure 5.5 only.)

5.3.1 Multiple indicators

In business studies, *multiple* indicators are often used to capture a given construct. For example, attitudes are often measured by multiple items combined into a scale. Why so? An example will clarify this. Assume that somebody is going to determine your mathematical skills. You get only one problem to solve. The outcome can be classified as 'correct' or 'false'. You will probably not be happy with the test. At best it can only reflect a modest fraction of your mathematical skills. Thus, a main reason for using multiple indicators is to create measurement which covers the domain of the construct which it purports to measure. Measures based on multiple indicators are also more robust, i.e. the random error in measurement is reduced.

In the research literature, the so-called Crohnbach's α is often reported. The Crohnbach's α can be conceived as a measure of the intercorrelations between the various indicators used to capture the underlying construct. The assumption is that the various indicators should correlate positively, but they should not be perfectly correlated. (If all

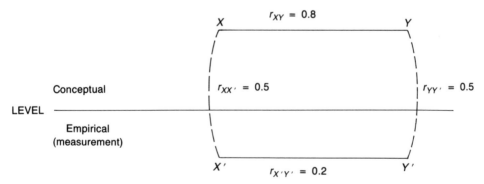

Figure 5.5 Measurement errors

the indicators were perfectly correlated, they would all capture exactly the same.) The underlying assumption is that one indicator only is inadequate to capture the construct. This way of reasoning refers to what is termed 'reflective' measurements, i.e. the various indicators are reflections of the underlying concept. This is in contrast to so-called formative measurement: elements which are supposed to map the underlying construct. An example is school performance measured as a sum of the grades obtained in the various subjects covered. In this case, there is no specific reason why the scores for the various subjects should correlate.

> You are supposed to measure the strategy followed by the competing firm in an industry of your choice. What do you think would be relevant indicators to capture the firm's strategies?

5.3.2   Construct validity

So far we have dealt with one aspect of validity or, more precisely, one aspect of *construct validity*. Construct validity is crucial and can be defined as 'the extent to which an operationalization measures the concept which it purports to measure' (Zaltman *et al.*, 1977: 44). Construct validity is necessary for meaningful and interpretable research findings and can be assessed in various ways:

- *Face validity* tells us to what extent the measure used seems to be a reasonable measure of what it purports to measure. A simple test for face validity is to ask for the opinion of others acquainted with the actual topic.
- *Convergent validity* tells us to what extent multiple measures and/or multiple methods yield similar (comparable) results. Correlational techniques are often used to assess convergent validity.
- *Divergent validity* tells us to what extent a construct is distinguishable from another construct. If a researcher measures, say, 'innovativeness', s/he should be confident of not measuring another construct, such as 'organizational resources'.

To assess convergent and divergent validity, the so-called multi-trait multi-method approach is often used (in addition to other methods, such as factor analysis). A very simple example is shown in Table 5.2 (which in no way demonstrates all aspects of the approach).

Table 5.2 is read as follows. A researcher has measured two constructs, X and Y, by two methods, M_1 and M_2. The table reports the correlation coefficients between the different measures. An inspection of the correlation coefficients for X and Y obtained by the two methods shows that $r = 0.82$ and $r = 0.79$, respectively. It is also seen that these correlation coefficients are substantially higher than any correlation coefficient between the X and Y measures.

Table 5.2 Two methods, two constructs

		M_1		M_2	
		X	Y	X	Y
M_1	X	1	0.35	0.82	0.27
	Y		1	0.30	0.79
M_2	X			1	0.29
	Y				1

As correlation coefficients for the same construct measured by different methods are high, and substantially higher than any between construct correlation coefficients, it is reasonable to assume convergent validity. Because the correlation coefficients between the constructs are modest, and substantially lower than the correlation coefficients for the same construct measured by different methods, we may conclude that convergent validity is present.

Going back to Table 5.2, it is also evident from using only one indicant or method for each construct that neither convergent nor discriminant validity can be assessed.

In a business study the following question was asked to assess a firm's competitiveness:

'How competitive is your firm?'

Not
competitive
at all

-3 -2 -1 0 1 2 3

Very
competitive

Do you think this is a valid way of measuring competitiveness? Why/why not?

5.3.3   Other forms of validity

Below is a brief discussion of three other forms of validity.

1. *Internal validity.* As emphasized in Chapter 4, researchers are often preoccupied with cause−effect relationships. Internal validity refers to the extent to which we can infer that a causal relationship exists between two (or more) variables.

A correlation between two variables does not, as such, indicate that there is a causal relationship, as it (the correlation coefficient) does not tell anything about direction or whether it is influenced by other factors (see section 4.3). However, even in correlational research we might be interested in knowing whether a correlation coefficient between two variables is 'true' without being concerned whether a causal relationship is present. Then, we need to control for and rule out the impact of other possible factors.

2. *Statistical conclusion validity.* In order to prove a causal relationship (or a covariation), it must also be statistically significant. Thus, statistical conclusion validity is a prerequisite for making inferences about causal relationships (and covariance).

To prove statistical conclusion validity, the study must be sufficiently sensitive. Statistical conclusion validity also relates to the question of 'effect size' and sample size needed. The impact of 'effect size' on statistical conclusion validity can be illustrated as follows. Assume that a researcher is willing to reject the null hypothesis and thus accept the alternative hypothesis if the findings are significant at the 5 per cent level or better.[3] In the present case, the researcher has hypothesized a positive relationship between income (X) and propensity to buy (Y). Based on previous findings, it is believed that the correlation coefficient between the two variables is close to $r_{XY} = 0.5$. For the case of simplicity, the researcher sets the critical value for rejecting the null hypothesis of the 5 per cent level ($\alpha = 0.05$) to $t = 2$. (Inspection of the t-distribution will show that it is influenced by a number of observations. As the number of observations increases, it approaches the normal distribution.)

From the formula, it can easily be calculated that the needed sample size is approximately

$$2 = 0.5\sqrt{n - 1}$$

$$\sqrt{n - 1} = \frac{2}{0.5} \approx 17$$

Inspecting the t-distribution once more shows that the required sample size is somewhat larger, as for $\alpha = 0.05$, $t > 2$. If, however, the assumed correlation between the two variables was $r = 0.10$, the number of observations needed is approximately 400! In the present case, the correlation coefficient between the two variables captures the notion of 'effect size'. From the above example, it is easily seen that the weaker the assumed relationship, the more observations are needed to demonstrate statistical conclusion validity.

A variety of factors may violate statistical conclusion validity, such as violating the assumptions underlying the statistical test(s) used. 'Fishing', i.e. searching for statistically significant findings (correlations) is also a threat to statistical conclusion validity. By chance, 'significant' findings may occur. For example, by *chance* five out of 100 correlation coefficients are expected to be significant at the 5 per cent level! Measurement errors may also be a threat to statistical conclusion validity (see Figure 5.5).

3. *External validity.* External validity relates to the extent to which findings can be generalized *to* particular persons, settings and times, as well as *across* types of persons, settings and times. For example, when conducting an election poll, external validity is usually used as a basis for generalizing the population of voters.

It should also be noted that, if the study lacks construct validity, the findings are *meaningless*, destroying also the internal and external validity of the findings!

5.4 Improving your measurements

In structured (descriptive and causal) research, but also in exploratory research, when one wants to examine potential relationships between variables (see section 4.2), one should proceed as follows:[4]

1. Start by elaborating the *conceptual definitions* and specifying the domain of constructs to be used. When dealing with practical problems, the point of departure should be the actual problem and how the problem can/should be represented (modelled) (cf. section 3.4). When the problem is represented, the constructs used to map the problem should be conceptually defined as a basis for subsequent operationalization.
2. Develop adequate *operational definitions* (measures). The researcher should inspect prior operationalizations/measurements used to capture the same constructs. In this phase, the researcher should also assess the face validity of the measurements, perhaps by experts critically examining the proposed measures.
3. *Correct* and *refine* the measures. Often multiple measurements are appropriate.
4. *Pre-test* the measures and evaluate their reliability and construct (convergent and discriminant) validity. This should be done before the next step.
5. Use the final measurement instrument in the study.

From the above discussion, it also follows that questionnaire design is closely related to measurement. The starting point is *what* information is needed. The information needed should, in structured research, be related to specific constructs: market size, competitive position and so on. These constructs must, as noted above, be adequately defined. Then the questions are designed to generate the needed information. An operational definition may consist of one or more questions.

Example
Market share for a producer of product X may be operationalized by the following sequence of questions among a random sample of potential buyers of a given product (which must be defined):

1. 'Do you use (product category) . . .'

___ Yes   ___ No

If *Yes*,

2. 'Do you remember the brand name of the product you use (last bought)?'

___ Yes   ___ No

If *Yes*,

3. 'What brand?' (brand mentioned)

One measure of market share (*MS*) is:

$$MS = \frac{\text{No. who mentioned X} \cdot 100}{\text{No. using the product}}$$

Careful examination of this measure (operational definition) will show that the measured market share rather reflects 'user share'. It should also be noted that this measure does not take into account variations in use quantity.

In the same way, if data are generated through observations, the procedures for obtaining the observations must be specified in detail. The specified procedures for making observations correspond to operational definitions are emphasized above.

5.5 Measurements in 'qualitative' research

The research literature deals only to a modest degree with measurement problems when it comes to exploratory/qualitative research. But is the question of measurement irrelevant in such research? The answer is probably *no*.

1. In Chapter 4 we saw that a key characteristic of exploratory research is that the problem under scrutiny is only partly understood. If the problem is only modestly understood, a prime purpose is to obtain understanding. A variety of approaches can be used (see Chapter 9 for a more detailed discussion). Assume that the researcher approaches the problem by using semi-structured questions, based on an interview guide (developed by surveying previous studies and so on). As noted above, a key purpose of measurements is to map 'reality'. When the researcher asks her or his questions, s/he gets responses (see Figure 5.6).

The responses R_1, R_2, ... are empirical manifestations which the researcher tries to understand. In this process s/he will try to relate this to her or his knowledge base and hopefully produce a reasonable explanation. This may partly be seen as 'data-driven' problem solving. However, without the use of concepts and theory, an explanation

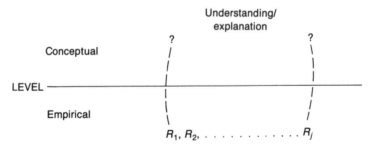

Figure 5.6 Responses and sense-making

(theory) will never emerge. Thus a mapping between empirical observations and concepts/theory is taking place. Besides noting that such research requires considerable conceptual skills, which is often overlooked, it should also be noted that the researcher should be able to demonstrate the validity of findings. In order to handle such validity claims, the researcher must supply evidence.[5] The researcher should report the questions, responses, inferences made and what supports these inferences. Thus, the *mapping*, *inferences* and *validity claims* have much in common with measurements, as discussed above.

An example will illustrate this point. Assume a medical doctor is examining a patient with the symptoms, $s_1, \ldots, s_n$. During the examination, the doctor arrives at a specific diagnosis and decides on treatment. Has the doctor made some sort of measurement? S/he has observed the symptoms and related them to her or his knowledge base, and thus conducted mapping between the observable symptoms and theory (diagnosis). An expert observer, who seldom or never makes diagnostic mistakes, makes *valid* mapping between empirical observations (symptoms) and theory (relevant diagnosis), which corresponds to excellent construct validity.

2. In business studies the researcher often makes use of secondary data. Such data are gathered by means of specific procedures, where specific measurements have been used as well. This indicates that, when using secondary data, one should *always* inspect and evaluate the data-gathering and measurement procedures used.

3. Analysis of written texts such as annual reports, business magazines and taped and transcribed interviews are often used in business research. Even here measurement problems are present. If the study is exploratory, the arguments put forward at the outset of this section (5.5) apply. If the research is structured (descriptive or causal), conceptual definitions must be developed and specific procedures (operational definitions) specified, as well as how the procedures should be applied, i.e. coding of the actual text.

The above discussion indicates that measurements are important and must be dealt with properly in research, where measurement problems have usually been given less attention.

Notes

1. For an excellent and entertaining demonstration, see Huff (1954).
2. For detailed discussion, see Cook and Campbell (1979).
3. For a discussion of hypothesis testing and the notion of significance, see any introductory textbook in statistics. A good discussion is also found in Churchill (1991).
4. For a more detailed overview, see Churchill (1979).
5. For an excellent discussion, see Kirk and Miller (1986).

CHAPTER 6

Data collection and sources

According to Oriental folklore, a man called Nasiruddin was searching for something on the ground. A friend stopped and asked, 'What have you lost, Nasiruddin?' 'My key,' replied Nasiruddin. The friend went down on his knees, trying to help, and they both looked for the key. After searching in vain for some time, the friend asked, 'Where exactly did you drop it?' 'In my house,' answered Nasiruddin. 'Then why are you looking here, Nasiruddin?' 'There is more light here than in my house,' replied Nasiruddin.

The purpose of this chapter is to look at: (1) what we mean by data collection, (2) what are the sources of data collection, (3) where to find the right data, and (4) how to collect data suitable for different types of study and research problem. Data sources are the carriers of data (information). A first distinction can be made between secondary and primary data sources. Secondary data are information collected by others for purposes which can be different from ours. Primary data are original data collected by us for the research problem at hand. These two types of data source are discussed in some detail.

6.1 Secondary data

Many research students underestimate the amount of data available from secondary sources. We should therefore start looking for secondary sources relevant to our research problem before going out to collect our own data.

A number of government offices regularly collect information on different aspects of our society. The census of population available in each country can provide us with an enormous amount of information on potential customers and segments in a society. The Central Bureau of Statistics and branch organizations collect information on different companies, their size and market shares, as well as imports and exports.

The following secondary sources can be important for our research (for a more comprehensive list, see Churchill, 1991):

- Central and local government studies and reports, census reports, state budgets, rules on international trade regarding imports and exports, and policies on foreign direct investment.
- Studies and reports of institutions and departments such as the Central Bureau of Statistics, universities, telecommunication departments, marketing and other research institutes, chambers of commerce and foreign missions such as embassies, trade centres and consulates.
- Academic as well as organizational journals and newsletters relevant to the problem area. In many countries, different branch organizations publish journals on statistics regarding their own industry, market shares, revenues and imports and exports.
- Historical studies regarding the development of a particular discipline or problem area.
- Textbooks and other published material directly or indirectly related to the problem area.
- And, last but not least, theses and reports written by other students in our own university and in other schools and universities. Many schools keep an up-to-date record of all the theses written in different disciplines. This is perhaps the most important secondary source at the earlier stages of our research process. They provide us with insight not only into our problem area, but also into the other sources mentioned above.

6.1.1 Advantages of secondary data

The first and foremost advantage of using secondary data is obviously the enormous saving in time and money. The researcher need only go to the library and locate and utilize the sources. This not only helps the researcher to formulate and understand the research problem better, but also broadens the base for which scientific conclusions can be drawn. In other words, the verification process is more rapid and the reliability of the information and conclusions is highly enhanced.

Another advantage of consulting secondary data is that it can suggest suitable methods or data to handle a particular research problem. Moreover, it provides a comparison instrument with which we can easily interpret and understand our primary data.

Considering all these advantages, many scholars recommend that all research should, in fact, start with secondary data sources. As put by Churchill (1987: 181): 'Do not bypass secondary data. Begin with secondary data, and only when the secondary data are exhausted or show diminishing returns, proceed to primary data.'

6.1.2 Disadvantages of secondary data

There are some serious drawbacks in working with secondary data. We should be careful in using data only because they are easily available and save us time and money. One of the main problems is that these data are collected for another study with different objectives and may not completely fit 'our' problem. It is therefore of the utmost importance to identify what we are studying, what we already know about the topic, and what we want to have as further information on the topic. Here we should make a list of the concepts on which we need to collect information. The idea is to take our research problem as the starting point for secondary data we need, and not the other way around.

It is sometimes difficult to classify these data in ways that are consistent with the study at hand. The variables might have been defined differently, or the measurement unit could have been totally different and would, therefore, make the comparison absolutely invalid. For example, when studying the export behaviour of smaller firms, we could use a number of studies undertaken in different countries and could compare the results with our findings. After a closer look, however, we might realize that 'smaller firms' were defined differently. To determine the size (small, medium or large), different measurement units were used. Some studies defined size in terms of sales, some in terms of number of employees, some in terms of profit and some in terms of square metres of occupied space as in the case of retailing firms.

Moreover, even if two studies use the same measurement unit, the terms of definition are often difficult. In a study in Norway, for example, firms with 200−499 employees were defined as medium-sized, while in the USA, firms with fewer than 500 employees were defined as smaller firms. In such a comparison, if the US study concluded that smaller firms depend highly on unsolicited orders for their initial export, we could not compare this finding with our findings in Norway by saying that: 'Consistent to the US study, smaller firms in Norway also depend heavily on unsolicited orders for their initial export while medium-sized firms are much more aggressive and do not depend upon unsolicited orders for their initial exports.'

These types of difference are quite common, and researchers using secondary data or comparing and supporting their findings with the help of these data should be aware of the problems and make the comparison with some caution. One way to ameliorate the situation is to discuss the differences and the relevance of secondary data with our own study, looking at the validity of comparison and how it should be understood.

Another problem is that it is the responsibility of the researcher that data are accurate; inaccuracies cannot be blamed on the secondary source. It is the researcher's responsibility to check whether findings presented by another researcher are based on primary or secondary data. It is therefore important always to check the original source of data. It is only the original source that can provide us with the required information on the quality of data because it describes the process of data collection and analysis.

One problem with accuracy is that we have to understand the purpose of data collection for the source we are using. For example, it is quite common for companies in their annual reports to utilize wishful thinking rather than facts when they describe market position. They may mention that they are market leaders or have a certain market share.

However, if we are studying the competitive position of a company, we should make certain checks to see whether it is the market leader or has the market share it claims.

6.2 Primary data

When secondary data are not available or are unable to help answer our research questions, we must ourselves collect the data which are relevant to our study and research problem. These data are called primary data. What we should look for, ask about and collect depends upon our research problem and research design. We have several choices as regards the means of collecting primary data. Normally, this includes observations, surveys (questionnaires) and interviews, as explained by Figure 6.1.

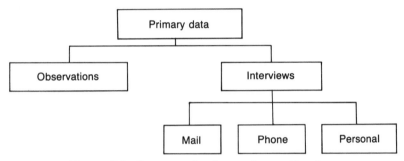

Figure 6.1 Sources of primary data collection

6.2.1 Observations

Observation as a data collection tool entails listening and watching other people's behaviour in a way that allows some type of analytical interpretation. The main advantage is that we can collect first-hand information in a natural setting. Moreover, we can interpret and understand the observed behaviour, attitude and situation more accurately, and capture the dynamics of social behaviour in a way that is not possible through questionnaires and interviews.

The main disadvantage is that most observations are made by individuals who systematically observe and record a phenomenon, and it is difficult to translate the events or happenings into scientifically useful information. This is particularly important when the purpose is to generalize from these observations. Here questions about validity and reliability become very important and need to be answered satisfactorily. When we collect data through observations, we have to make a number of choices regarding, for example, participatory versus non-participatory, lab versus fieldsettings, etc. This is further illustrated by Figure 6.2.

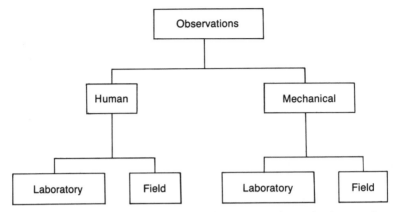

Figure 6.2 Choices for collecting primary data through observations

In participant or field observation, the observer is a natural part of the situation or event. The researcher is a part of a company or organization and decides to study the same organization in one way or another. Sometimes a researcher specifically joins an organization to be able to observe as a participant. In other words, in this case the observation is not hidden or disguised: people who are being observed know that they are being observed and by whom. In business studies, participant observation can enable researchers to have access to what people actually do instead of what they might claim they do (the difference between formal and informal organization). One danger of participatory observation is that the observers can be so influenced by the event, situation or culture and everyday lives of the subjects that they become unable to take a neutral view of events and situations. On the other hand, observers can be so ethnocentric that they are not able to observe or analyze the situation because they believe the subjects have an inferior culture or that the observer knows best (Douglas, 1976).

In non-participant observations, the observer or researcher observes a natural setting but is not part of the situation her/himself. It has been reported in several studies that the behaviour of people is influenced by the presence of a non-participatory observer, but only in the beginning and that people get used to it in a very short time. One way to overcome this problem is to observe under disguise. For example, in a buying/selling situation an observer can act as a potential customer.

As mentioned earlier, observation as a data collection method should not be selected because it is easier. This choice is highly influenced by the research problem, research design, researcher's skills, capabilities and nature, and the characteristics of the subject to be observed.

6.2.2 Surveys and questionnaires

Surveys and questionnaires are the most popular data collection method in business studies, and the major types of questionnaire are descriptive and/or analytical. Once a

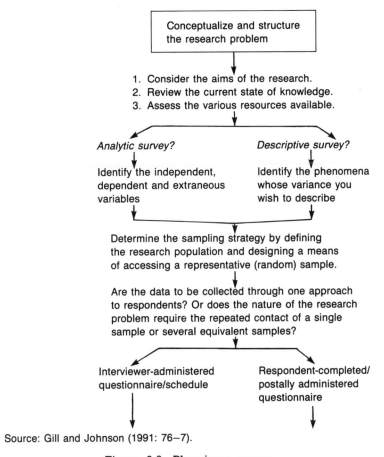

Source: Gill and Johnson (1991: 76–7).

Figure 6.3 Planning a survey

research problem is formulated and the purpose of the study is clearly defined, this will determine the type of survey we should undertake, whether analytical or descriptive. Different surveys lead to different problems and issues, and demand different types of planning and handling. According to Gill and Johnson (1991), the planning of a survey should follow the pattern suggested by Figure 6.3.

According to Simons (1987), with analytical surveys we can test a theory by taking the logic into the field: for example, to understand the relationship between accounting control systems and business strategy. Thus, in this type of survey, we have to emphasize specifying the independent, dependent and extraneous variables. We should also give due attention to and benefit from existing literature, theory and research while conceptualizing and structuring our own research. The review of literature is therefore of the utmost importance. In analytical surveys, independent, dependent and extraneous variables are controlled through statistical techniques such as multiple regression. The questions and variables included in such a survey thus need careful conceptualization and measurement scales.

On the other hand, descriptive surveys are concerned with identifying the phenomena whose variance we wish to describe. The survey is concerned with particular characteristics of a specific population of subjects, either at a fixed point in time or at varying times for comparative purposes. Here the focus is more on a representative sample of the relevant population than on the analytical design, as we are concerned principally with the accuracy of the findings and their generalizability. Even in these surveys, a review of earlier research and literature is important to determine what kind of questions are to be included in the questionnaire. In business studies, descriptive surveys are often used to obtain consumer attitudes towards a certain product and to ascertain views and opinions of employees in an organization (Reeves and Harper, 1981). These surveys are often used to understand the behaviour of employees as regards motivation, job satisfaction and grievances.

Figure 6.3 also illustrates that both analytical and descriptive surveys are concerned with identifying the population (object of the study). The population would provide all the responses which would help us to answer our research questions. From this population a sample should be drawn that is representative. Sampling is treated separately in this book as it is an important part of research activity. The research problem and objectives would also dictate whether or not data are to be collected by only one approach, or whether we have to contact our sample again and again. In either case, we have to consider practicalities and access before starting work on a questionnaire and schedule (Moser and Kalton, 1971).

Finally, we have to decide whether we are going to send the questionnaire by mail and wait for the answers, or whether we should interview the respondent face to face or by telephone. Here not only the research problem and objectives, but also issues such as sample size, location, availability of funds and complexity of information required, may influence the procedure and schedule. Resources are very important at this stage. For example, postal surveys are generally less expensive and time consuming than personal interviews. Moreover, in postal surveys there is a high rate of 'non-response', while in interviews there is a risk of interviewer bias (Scott, 1961; Boyd and Westfall, 1970).

The first step in the construction of a questionnaire is to specify what type of information is required. This depends, first, on the type of study we have at hand. In the case of descriptive and causal studies, we should have knowledge on the basis of hypotheses and propositions. We should know what is the basis of our study and what we want to achieve. Here we should also consider to whom this questionnaire is to be sent and what is to be asked. For example, in exploratory studies, we should have an unstructured questionnaire.

Second, we should consider whether the questionnaire is going to be disguised or undisguised. Moreover, we must consider how it is to be administered — through mail, personal interview, telephone interview or a combination of the above.

Third, we should consider the construction of individual questions. Is it necessary to ask a certain question? What are the benefits of dummy variables and tables? Is it necessary to have several questions on one issue? Can questions be interpreted differently? Would respondents be willing to give answers to the questions? How long would it take for them to answer? Would they be in a position to answer a particular question? Is it a sensitive issue? All questions based on a questionnaire should be judged according to the above.

Fourth, we should consider how the questions are to be answered. Should we have open-ended questions such as: 'How old are you?' and 'What is the total turnover of your company?' where no answers or alternatives to a question are provided and respondents can answer exactly as they like? Or should we have closed questions such as: 'How old are you? Please tick the appropriate box below' (see Figure 6.4)? With open-ended questions, we may end up with enormous variations in answers that would make coding or categorization difficult or almost impossible. On the other hand, we can get correct answers from the respondents when they do not have to limit their answers to one of the categories mentioned in Figure 6.4. We should, therefore, be aware of the type of information we need to have for each question, so that we can formulate the questions and expected answers accordingly.

Another aspect that should be considered here is whether or not we should have 'Don't know' or 'No comment' alternatives. In this case, we might be providing an escape route to a respondent wanting to avoid answering a question, perhaps due to its sensitive nature.

The length of questionnaires and its effect on the response rate and responses is important. A common belief is that the shorter the questionnaire, the higher the chance that it will be returned fully completed. However, there are no standards available in the existing literature regarding what is a 'short' and what is a 'long' questionnaire. The idea is that a respondent gets tired or loses interest in answering the questions as the length increases. Some guidelines for designing questionnaires are presented in the following section.

The precise wording of questions is crucial in achieving maximum validity of survey information (data) collected through asking questions. This is illustrated by the following story (Sudman and Bradburn, 1989: 8):

Two priests, a Dominican and a Jesuit, are discussing whether it is a sin to smoke and pray at the same time. After failing to reach a conclusion, each goes off to consult his

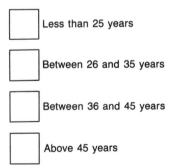

Figure 6.4 Categories for closed questions

Strongly agree	Agree	Partly agree	Disagree	Strongly disagree
☐	☐	☐	☐	☐

Figure 6.5 Scale for ranking answers

respective superior. The next week they meet again. The Dominican says, 'Well, what did your superior say?' The Jesuit responds, 'He said it was all right.' 'That's funny,' the Dominican replies, 'my superior said it was a sin.' Jesuit: 'What did you ask him?' Reply: 'I asked him if it was all right to smoke while praying.' 'Oh,' said the Jesuit, 'I asked my superior if it was all right to pray while smoking.'

The above story reveals that a small change in wording can cause large differences in the meaning and responses. At this stage, we should also decide whether we should have 'Yes' and 'No' questions, where the respondent has to take a position. Moreover, in questions where the respondent has to rank answers, we need to decide what type of scale we should use. For example, should we use the scale shown in Figure 6.5 or say: 'Please rank your answer on the scale of 1 to 10, where 10 is the most important or positive'?

Considering the above, we provide some guidelines for the construction of questionnaires.

1. The questions must be asked in a very *simple and concise language.* Here one should consider the respondent when it comes to educational level, background, knowledge and acquaintance with the subject matter. The questions should then be adjusted and adapted to the above-mentioned characteristics of the respondents. Not only the questions but also the alternative answers provided (in the case of closed questions) should use a clear and unambiguous language.

2. In this connection, we should be rather conservative as to the level of knowledge, education, etc. necessary for the respondent to answer the question. *No unrealistic demand* should be made on the respondent's know-how, memory and willingness to respond.

3. We should check and ensure that everybody *understands the question in the same manner*: in other words, that everybody draws the same meaning from the questions. This is particularly important in questions or questionnaires which are translated from one language to another. One way to deal with this is to have an expert translate the questions, for example, from English to Norwegian, and then have another expert translate the text back from Norwegian to English. The researcher can then clearly see if there has been any change in the meaning. The discrepancies should be corrected with the help of experts from both sides.

4. Each question should deal with only *one dimension* or aspect. If we mix up several dimensions or aspects of questions in one question, it will be difficult for respondents to explain their behaviour or to answer 'yes' or 'no'. In other words, one cannot ask one question about more than one variable or dimension of the study. Each variable and dimension should be covered by a separate question. It is quite common to ask several questions on one variable or to have each question cover different dimensions of the subject matter.

In other words, *avoid 'double-barrelled' questions*, such as: 'What is the turnover of your company and how much of that comes from export?' or 'What is your educational background and how long have you been working in this position?' One way to do this is not to use 'and' in any question.

5. The questions should be formulated in such a way that there is *no escape route* in the questions. We should not offer an alternative such as 'Don't know' or 'No comment' (see Figure 6.6).

Moreover, the questions should be *specific and concise*, and not too general in nature so that the respondent does not give several answers. If we must have some general questions, we should check the understanding of these questions through another question. The more specific and concise the questions are, the easier it is for us to interpret these questions and answers in different categories and then draw conclusions.

The questions should *not be of a suggestive nature*, directing the respondent towards an answer or a specific opinion. For example, we should not ask a high-tech company the following question: 'Do you consider R & D important for your type of company?'

6. Questions should be formulated in a *polite and soft language*. They should not irritate, offend or provoke the respondent. It is very important to place the sensitive questions, if any, at the right place in the questionnaire, so that the respondent can understand why that particular question is being asked. In some cases, it is necessary to have these 'understanding' questions first. But, in any case, there must be a logical and systematic sequence of questions to avoid misunderstandings and to ensure a high response rate. We must keep in mind that the respondent, by answering the questions, is doing us a favour.

7. The language and words used in the questions should be *straightforward* and should not have double meanings, otherwise the respondent will answer the questions with a different understanding and will thereby contribute negatively to the conclusions of the

'Who are the primary users of your exported products/services?'

☐ Industry ☐ Consumers

☐ Government ☐ Don't know

'Do you consider exporting is or will be a major business activity of your company?'

☐ Yes ☐ No ☐ Don't know or No comment

Figure 6.6 Examples of escape routes

study. Another risk is that the respondent, if not sure of the question's meaning, will leave the question unanswered. For example, it will be quite difficult for a respondent to understand what you want to know by the following question: 'What type of structure does your company have for export activities?' or 'What are the major barriers to entry faced by your company in the international market?'

If one is using complex wording or concepts, a note describing or clarifying the exact meaning of the text should be added to the question. Several authors (e.g. Cannell *et al.*, 1981) have advocated that an explanation or argument as to why that particular question is being asked gives a better response rate.

8. Questions should be placed in a *'right' order*. The easy-to-answer questions and positive types of question should be placed first. If we place the complicated or difficult questions first — for example, questions for which the respondents need to consult books or managers/colleagues — they might get the impression that all the questions are of that nature and thus refrain from responding at all. The same is true for sensitive questions. There should also be a logical sequential order from general to specific questions.

9. The layout of the questionnaire is also important. It should look *neat and tidy* as this can influence the respondents' willingness to answer.

10. Last but not least, we should go through the questionnaire critically or have a friend, colleague or adviser go through it critically and give comments. The best way to do this is to do a *pre-test* on 3–5 real companies or respondents. In such a pre-test, we should check whether the above-mentioned issues such as understanding, the level of difficulty, the willingness to answer sensitive questions and the time it takes to answer the questionnaire are as we wish.

> We should realize that the respondent is doing us a favour by replying to our questions.

6.2.3   Interviews

In research we use two types of interview. The first type is survey research interviews, where a standard format of interview is used with an emphasis on fixed response categories and systematic sampling, and loading procedures combined with quantitative measures and statistical methods. The second type is unstructured interviews, where the respondent is given almost full liberty to discuss reactions, opinions and behaviour on a particular issue. The interviewer is there just to give lead questions and to record the responses in order later to understand 'how' and 'why'. The questions and answers are unstructured and are not systematically coded beforehand.

In the literature there is some discussion of semi-structured interviews, which differ from an unstructured and a structured interview. They differ from unstructured interviews as topic and issues to be covered, sample size, people to be interviewed, and questions to be asked have been determined beforehand. They also differ in the way in

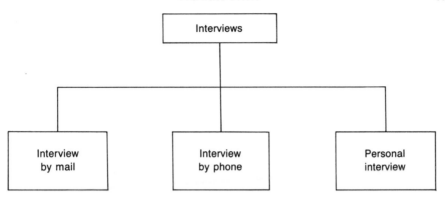

Figure 6.7   A typology of interviews

which we plan to minimize bias. In semi-structured interviews, we handle bias by careful design of the technique itself: bias arising from the sequence in which we address subject matter, from any inadvertent omission of questions, from unrepresentative sampling and from an uncontrolled over- or under-representation of subgroups among our respondents. Semi-structured and unstructured interviews differ from structured interviews in that they demand greater skills from the interviewer than the fully structured interviews. In semi-structured and unstructured interviews, we often obtain information about personnel, and attitudinal and value-laden material, and we are likely to be dealing with matters which call for social sensitivity in their own right (Jankowicz, 1991).

There is an abundance of literature available on standardized versus unstandardized or semi-structural interviews when it comes to the question form and respondent understanding (e.g. Schumann and Presser, 1976; Beza, 1984; Mishler, 1986; Fowler and Mangione, 1990). Anybody interested in this subject should consult any of the above volumes. Our purpose here is not to involve ourselves in this discussion, but to provide some guidelines for interviewing. A typology of interviews is provided in Figure 6.7.

For the purpose of this volume, interviews refer to face-to-face verbal exchanges, in which one person, the interviewer, attempts to acquire information or opinions or beliefs from another person, the interviewee.

The *advantage* of in-depth interviews is that we can have a more accurate and clear picture of a respondent's position or behaviour. This is possible because of open-ended questions and because respondents are free to answer according to their own thinking, as we have not constrained answers by a few alternatives. This is also true in the case of complicated or sensitive issues, where the interviewer can ask for further elaboration of answers and attitudes. This method of data collection is highly suitable for exploratory and inductive types of study as it matches very well with the purposes of these studies.

The *disadvantage* related to in-depth interviews is that they demand a skilled and cautious interviewer. The interviewer should have a complete understanding of the research problem, its purpose and what information we are looking for. The course of the interview is decided by the skills of the interviewer when asking questions and probing further with supplementary questions. The know-how and skills of the interviewer are thus of the utmost importance. Interviews can also take a long time — longer than filling in structured questionnaires — and may even require several interviews with the same respondent (Churchill, 1987). In addition, interviews are also difficult to interpret and analyze. Our own background may highly influence the interpretations, thereby causing problems of objectivity. Depending upon which type of analysis we want to do, coding of in-depth interviews is a difficult task in spite of improved coding techniques and systems.

6.2.4 Preparing for an interview

The first steps in preparing for an interview are to: (1) analyze your research problem, (2) understand what information you really need to have from an interviewee, and (3) see who would be able to provide you with that information (see also Chapter 3). The clearer the problem statement is, the easier it is to know what to ask. It is understood that the purpose of data collection through interviews is to obtain valid information from the most appropriate person. In other words, you should clearly know what you want to ask as well as who are the persons who can provide the most relevant and valid information on those issues (Buckley, 1983). Moreover, the interviewee should be willing to answer your questions truthfully. For example, you cannot expect people to be honest on very sensitive matters. These are some of the issues you must keep in mind while preparing for interviews.

The next step is to draft an *interview guide or interview questions*. These questions should be compared with the research problem several times, partly to test the consistency between the two and partly to see whether the questions are thorough and correct enough to find out what you want. It is very useful to let somebody else (perhaps your adviser) see the problem statement and the questions to be asked in the interview to check this congruence.

After the above scrutiny, a first draft of the interview questions should be prepared. This draft has to be pre-tested as *a pilot study*. While the above scrutiny dealt with the researcher's understanding of the research problem and the interview questions, the test checks the understanding of the interviewee regarding the research problem and interview questions. Such pilot research also provides first-hand insight into what might be called the 'cultural endowment' of the informants. After this pilot study, where a couple of respondents have been asked to read the research problem and the interview questions, and have also answered the questions and have commented on the understanding of questions, you can prepare the final draft of the interview guide and questions.

Here, particular attention has to be given to the approach you are going to use: for instance, before contacting the interviewee you have to decide *how much time* the interview should take. The pilot study can help you to determine the time needed for your questions. You must consider that business executives work with the belief that 'Time is money' and might refuse to offer an interview only because of the shortage of time. Our experience shows that an interview should not take more than one and a half hours; ideally, it should take around one hour. However, the total meeting time can be two hours or more. In many cases, the interview is preceded or followed by a factory visit or lunch.

In open-ended interviews you can get a lot of information during the factory visit or lunch.

In this respect it is very important to realize that the interviewer has to *create a situation* where the respondent willingly offers time. If the respondent is not sufficiently motivated to provide you with time, there will be little motivation to answer your questions and to be an interviewee. This can jeopardize the whole purpose of the interview.

Once you have considered all aspects and *prepared the interview guide*, you should approach the person(s) you want to interview. Here you can use the telephone or a letter, perhaps both. In the letter, for example, you can explain the purpose of your study, provide a short problem statement and describe the type of information you are interested in collecting. In this letter you may also mention that you will be calling very soon (next Monday, next week, etc.) to request an appointment for an interview. In the letter or telephone call you should also mention how much time you think the interview will take. You must remember that you cannot demand a certain time, day or week for the interview: you have to adapt to the interviewee's schedule and not the other way around.

One important issue which you have to clear before you contact the interviewee is how you are going to *record the information* you will get. There has been a lot of discussion on the methods of recording information and it is widely accepted that tape-recording is a useful method. The disadvantages with recording are that the respondent might hesitate or even not answer some questions which are sensitive. Moreover, there is a risk that, while tape-recording, the interviewer might cease to listen carefully, believing that all the information is going on a tape which will be listened to later in a more relaxed environment. It is therefore recommended that some note taking, together with tape-recording, is most useful (see Lofland, 1971, for further discussion).

When you make the approach for an appointment, you will have to *inform the respondent* whether or not you will be using tape or video recorders. In fact, instead of informing, you should ask whether or not you can use the tape recorder. This issue automatically leads to the question of *confidentiality*. You will have to ask if the interview is to be treated confidentially and you will have to give your promise (undertaking or personal guarantee) that all information you receive will be kept confidential. If necessary, you may send a written assurance of confidentiality, signed by yourself and perhaps your adviser or any other responsible person from the school — for example, the director of research.

When making an appointment, you should also remember that you have *to create a reason or a reward* for the respondent — why should they answer your question? What is in it for them? For example, you can mention that the result of the study will be provided to the respondent, or that these results might help in analyzing a competitive/managerial position: that he/she/the company in question would benefit from the study. Or perhaps the study would help the industry or the country as a whole, or help the policy-makers in their job and thereby indirectly the firm in question. As mentioned earlier, the interviewee has to be motivated.

Now that you have the appointment, it is time to decide who is going to interview: one person or more, the same person doing all the interviews, or different people interviewing different companies/managers. If several interviewers are used, they have to be trained. In standardized interviewing, where it is common to use a number of people as interviewers, each interviewer has to be trained. Once you have taken an appointment and cleared matters such as the amount of time to be used, tape-recording or not, etc., you should send a *confirmation letter* about the appointment, thanking the interviewee for giving you an opportunity to come and visit them and saying you look forward to seeing them on the agreed date. This is necessary to avoid any misunderstandings on date or timing, and also to remind the interviewee.

Before closing the preparation section, we would like to discuss what you need to do before you start making appointments and interviewing. It is very important to analyze, discuss and consider *resources available* to you for performing these interviews. You have to consider all the costs: for example, travelling costs, the time for the interviews and also the time you need to process the interviews. We have seen a number of examples where the researchers start a very ambitious interview process and after a couple of interviews, or after about 50 per cent of their planned interviews, they give up due to travelling expenses, the time consumed or loss of interest. We have seen several students start their research interviewing by spending $2-4$ hours at each interview, tape-recording everything and ending up with several hours of recorded tape. But when they started listening to the tapes, which is a very time-consuming and tedious job, they did not know what to do with them all, and in fact reported that they had used less than half of the interviews they had recorded. The best way to handle this issue is to discuss these matters with your adviser before you start interviewing.

Prepare and pre-test your interview guide or questions.

6.2.5 Pre-interview

The appointment has been made with the respondent and now you have to review the questionnaire together with your supervisor. Here you must consider the data collection dimension: how you are going to use the responses for the analysis in your report, and how you want to present the information you are gathering. You also have to schedule your time properly. If you are having more than one interview per day, you should *plan your time*. This is particularly important when you are in a foreign environment or if you are in another city, as you must also consider how much time you need to arrive at the location from your hotel. The interviewees, business executives, have limited time and are always very busy. If you have already informed them that you need one hour of their time, you cannot come half an hour late and give an excuse that it took longer to arrive than you thought, or that you were stuck in traffic or could not find a taxi.

Another important issue is one of *social conventions*, meaning how you behave in the interviews, what type of dress you should have and so on. It is advisable to be 'proper'. If you go in shabby clothes and worn-out jeans, you may not give a positive impression to the interviewee as regards your seriousness and the fact that you can do worthwhile research and thereby may be of some help to the company. It is also wise not to 'party' the night before. It would not be very nice to go for an interview smelling of alcohol or half asleep.

Finally, we believe that interviewing is a skill you should *rehearse or practise* with regard to understanding, time to be consumed, your own arguments and questions, etc. You may find a 'victim' such as a friend and practise the interview. If there is the slightest risk that the respondent may misunderstand something, then they probably will. Moreover, it goes without saying that you much check and recheck the equipment you are going to use in the interview, such as the tape recorder or video recorder.

Dress properly and check your timing, questions and recording material.

6.2.6   The interview

The first important issue here is to introduce the study and its purpose and *to orient the respondents*. The interviewer should be able to answer clearly all the questions the respondents might have, such as: Who will benefit from the study? When will the final report be ready? Will they get a report or not? Moreover, the interviewer should reinforce the confidentiality, if required, to the respondent's satisfaction. At this stage, it is important to realize that the respondent is asking the questions and the interviewer has to provide satisfactory answers. These introductory 5 − 10 minutes can be a determining factor in how the rest of the interview goes.

The language used in these early minutes and in the subsequent interaction is of great importance. The interviewer has to use a *simple and understandable language*, being extra careful when using a certain terminology or concepts from a particular discipline, such as finance or management. It is quite possible that business executives, although they might have been working in the field for several years, will not be familiar with textbook terminology. This point is even more important when the interview is taking place in another environment or country. In that case, it is not only the terminology you have to be careful about, but also the language as a whole. You have to be sure that the language and the level of language you are using is compatible with the respondent's knowledge and usage of the same language.

The interviewer, irrespective of questioning technique, must leave it entirely to the *informant to provide answers* to questions. In other words, the questions should not be asked in a leading or directive manner as this pressures the respondent to answer in one particular way or even to give the answer s/he thinks you want to have. For example, do not pose questions such as: 'You must have realized that . . .' or 'How could you . . .'. Moreover, it is important that the interviewer, every now and then, expresses an understanding of what the interviewee is saying. A nodding of the head or a 'h'm' from time to time gives the impression that the interviewer understands what is meant. For the interviewee to keep on asking and answering questions, the interviewer has to show interest and enthusiasm in the respondents and their 'story'.

Although it is advised that interviewees are given full freedom to express personal meanings and give their own answers, it is quite important that the interviewer controls the situation so as to get the relevant information (relevant, that is, to the research area). Therefore, *control with some care* is necessary, not only to get the relevant information but also to manage the time. The interviewee has to be given reasonable time for each question and should not be interrupted every now and then. However, business executives or other respondents often like to talk at length about their experiences and know-how, especially about positive events, and should therefore be controlled, but with care.

Controlling time is very important, as the interviewee has given you a certain time and may be interested in talking a lot on each and every issue. You must ensure that you have answers to all of your questions within the specified time. If the time agreed upon beforehand was between 09.00 and 10.30, it is quite possible that at 10.30 the interviewee has to go to a meeting, just stops talking and asks you to leave, or a number of people enter the room to have a meeting, giving you only the option of leaving.

You also have to, in a way, *develop a relationship* with the interviewee. That is why we stress taking great care in the opening minutes of the interview. You must be able to give an impression of a serious, trustworthy and friendly person. The relationship can also be developed by expressing interest in the interviewee's position and opinion, and by appreciating his/her point of view. The better the relationship between the interviewer and the interviewee, the more open the relationship and the more useful the information you get. This is also important in case you have not been able to get all the information, due to time or any other reason, or if you would like to have some additional information later on. If the interviewee enjoyed talking to you, s/he would probably not mind having another meeting with you. As mentioned earlier, the interview is quite often combined with a factory visit or lunch. These are excellent opportunities to develop trust, friendship and a positive relationship with the interviewee.

You should be *careful about sensitive questions*. Many times it is just a matter of phrasing or using the right language to make the questions less sensitive. Sometimes, the questions are of a sensitive nature but still must be asked. Here the interviewee should not be pressured to provide a definite yes or no (admit it) answer. Questions regarding why a certain strategy or plan failed, about competitors and their success or about some financial issues can be of this nature. For example, while interviewing a bank manager the following question can be quite sensitive: 'Who is responsible for all the bad debts reported by your branch/office?' The same question can be asked in another way. For example: 'What, in your opinion, are the factors that caused the bad debts reported by your branch/office?' It is also advisable to avoid direct questions on who was responsible for a certain blunder or miscalculation. Questions regarding intra-organizational conflicts should be asked with some care and with indirect language.

Asking respondents for other sources of information can give an impression that you are not satisfied with their answers or that the answers have not fulfilled your expectations, and that you therefore need to know where you can get better answers. It can also give the impression that you have not done your homework properly and do not know the sources of relevant information for your study.

The previous section discussed recording of interviews. As mentioned earlier, if you are recording the interview on tape or video, the most important issue is that the equipment functions at the time of the interview. If it does not, you may give a very bad impression to the respondent. We said earlier that, even if you are using tape or video, it is best to take some notes as well. This not only records very crucial points twice, but also demonstrates interest and keeps you awake and alert.

> Develop a positive relationship with the interviewee and be prepared.

6.2.7 Post-interview

After coming back from the interview, you should *write down the important points* from the interview as well as notes on the practical details. This can include whether you were able to get all the answers or how much time it took, some opinions on the respondent, such as a very open or reserved person, and also your perception of your interaction and relationship with the interviewee. All these details will help you later on when you listen to the recorded tape or when you sit down to write the information you collected. Most of all, it will help you in case you need to have additional information. If the interview was not recorded, it is recommended that you go through the notes and write a complete, descriptive report of the interview immediately (or as soon as possible) after the interview. There is a great risk that you might forget many crucial points if you wait too long. The risk is particularly high if you are doing several interviews, as then you might even mix things up.

The second thing you have to do is to write a *'thank you' letter* to the respondent. You may also send some further information on your research project which you might have promised or realized in the interview that they would like to have. You should always try to maintain the relationship and keep the respondent informed about the progress of the study.

> Send a letter of thanks and maintain the relationship.

Reporting or transcribing an interview is an important and tedious job. As mentioned earlier, interviews which are not recorded should be written as a narrative story as soon as possible. For structured interviews, you should check your forms to see if they are completely and properly filled in. The interviews which are recorded always need some supporting material to remind you of the situation and the feeling of the interview. The best way is first to write down all the information on the tape in the same order, and later to develop a descriptive report of the interview relevant for the study. In this second stage you can discard all irrelevant talk and information.

Sometimes it is useful to send this descriptive report to the interviewee for comments. You might have misunderstood something or perhaps are not sure about what the respondent really wanted to say. Depending upon your relationship with interviewees, they might like to see what they said and, quite often, they give additional information or clarify their message voluntarily. In fact, many times they demand to see the report before you can use it. It is also important for trust and for ensuring confidentiality or sensitivity that the interviewee has a chance to see what information you believe you will be using in your study.

As we analyze the material collected through different methods, we realize that some material is superfluous and need not be included, while some sections need to be fleshed out and require more details.

> Go promptly through your interview notes.

CHAPTER 7

Sampling

7.1 Why take a sample? Basic concepts

In an election poll, only a small fraction of the voters are asked about their voting intentions, even though the pollsters' ultimate interest is in the opinions of the complete collection of persons eligible for voting. Using statistical terms, each voter is called a *unit*, the voters actually polled are called a *sample* and the collection of all persons eligible for voting is called the *population*. The alternative candidates in a presidential election can be considered as *values* of the *variable* 'candidate'. It would even be correct, but unusual, to say that the candidate who receives the majority of the votes in the population is a *parameter*. The whole process of obtaining results this way is called *sampling*. Sampling is very useful in business research and can be used in a variety of ways.

In the preceding sections we explained how to interview the chief business executive of a firm within a certain industry. The *unit* here is the executive or the firm. Very often a research problem is structured in such a way that you would like to hear the opinions of *all* the units within the population, which here is the industry. To do this would be *extremely time consuming and expensive*. Therefore, we usually interview only a smaller collection of chief business executives, called a *sample*. The number of units included in the sample is called the *sample size* and is commonly denoted by n. If our objective is to find out what is typical for the industry as a whole, it is important that the executives we interview are leaders of firms which are representative of the population.

> Sampling means saving work by examining the sample instead of the whole population.

7.2 Probability and non-probability sampling

Several *sampling designs*, i.e. methods of drawing the sample, are available. A sampling design is a special kind of *research design* or a part of a research design. Research designs in general are treated in Chapter 4. Sampling designs can be divided into probability sampling and non-probability sampling designs. In a *non-probability sample*, the probability that a particular unit will be included in the sample is unknown. In a *probability sample*, all units have known, but not necessarily equal, probabilities of being included.

Examples of non-probability samples are as follows:

- In a *convenience sample*, units that we find convenient for some reason are selected. We could, for instance, interview the chief business executives we happen to know personally.
- In a *judgement sample*, judgement is used to try to get a sample which is representative of the population. We simply try to select units we think are representative of the population.
- In a *quota sample*, we just make sure that certain subgroups of units, like small firms, intermediate firms and large firms, are represented in the sample in approximately the same proportions as they are represented in the population. (For further discussion, see Churchill, 1991: 539−44.)

Non-probability samples are easy to draw, but they may give misleading results if they, in spite of our judgement, happen to be unrepresentative of the population. The major drawback of non-probability samples is that such samples give no basis for evaluating the size of the *sampling variation* and the *error of estimation*.

If possible, we should therefore use a probability sample. This is especially important if we want to estimate unknown parameters or draw valid inferences regarding the population on the basis of the sample. In scientific research, non-probability samples are not very useful in the final analysis. But at early stages in a research process, such samples may give new insights and form the basis for new hypotheses.

> The sampling design should result in valid and reliable inferences for the population at a low cost.

7.3   Simple random sampling: an example

The following is an example of the process of sampling, using simple random sampling.

Example
Suppose we want to estimate the total amount of money budgeted for research and development (R & D) next year within a certain industry. How should we go about doing this?

First, we should remember that sampling is an expensive and demanding activity. Careful planning is necessary. Several questions need to be answered.

1. *What is the basic unit to be examined or interviewed?* In our example, *each firm* is the natural unit to use. In general, the unit could be a person, a household, an organization, a ship, an apartment, a county or almost anything, depending on the kind of investigation that is planned.

2. *How should the population be delimited?* The population or, more precisely, *the target population* is defined as the collection of units for which the research results are intended to be valid. In our example, the population is the collection of *all firms in the industry*. This delimitation may have to be refined, however. What is the minimum size for a firm to be included? What about firms operating within several industries? What about plants located abroad? For practical reasons, the population we decide to use, called *the sampled population*, may be somewhat different from the target population. This difference is a potential validity threat, if too large. The number of units in the sampled population is called the *population size* and is commonly denoted by N. We assume here that N is a finite number. Most probability sampling designs require that N is known.

3. *What variables or parameters are of interest?* Research results are very often expressed in terms of variables or parameters. *Parameters* describe aspects of variables. The population can be described in terms of variables or parameters. A *variable* can be defined as a set of values related to a population in such a way that each unit has one and only one value from the set. In our example, the amount budgeted for R & D as it varies in the population is a variable. A *value* can be defined as a piece of information regarding a particular aspect of a unit. In our example, the R & D figure for a specific firm is the value for that firm. Other aspects of variables are treated in Appendix A.

The parameter of interest in our example is a *population total*, namely the total of the budgeted R & D figures for the whole population. Other typical parameters to be estimated in a sampling survey in general are *population means*, *population proportions*, *population variances* and *population ratios*. Thus, in our example we could be interested in the *mean* R & D figure for the whole population, or the *proportion* of firms in the population having R & D figures smaller than a certain limit, or the *variance* of the R & D figures in the population, or the *ratio* of R & D expenditures to profits for the industry as a whole. When more than one variable is involved, additional parameters of interest might be *population correlation coefficients* and *population regression coefficients*. A *demand elasticity*, which can be derived from a population regression coefficient, can also be denoted a parameter.

> Research results are often expressed in terms of parameter estimates.

4. *How should one go about drawing the sample?* This is a question of sampling design. Several designs are available in the literature on sampling. The simplest design for drawing a probability sample is called *simple random sampling*. We will describe this for our example. A simple random sample of size n is a sample drawn by a method assuring that all conceivable samples of size n have had the same probability of being drawn. It can be shown that a random sample is obtained if we make sure that all the units

Table 7.1 Abbreviated example of a data matrix

Firm number	Profits	Budgeted R & D expenditure
1	− 302	30
2	6976	349
3	958	144
4	530	186
5	4709	1177
6	2594	830
7	− 1248	112
8	8072	969
9	− 241	29
10	7442	1042

in the population have the same probability of being drawn. One *method* of getting a random sample of size n from a population of size N is thus to put N labels in a hat and to draw n of them at random. Usually more sophisticated methods involving tables of random digits or computer programs are used.

Suppose that in our example there are $N = 900$ firms in the population and that we want to take a random sample of $n = 60$ firms. Then we must provide a list where all the firms have been numbered from 1 to 900. Such a list is called a *frame*. Next we use a computer program to generate 60 random figures between 1 and 900. Alternatively, we can use three columns from a table of random digits. Reading down the page from an arbitrary starting point, we list all figures smaller than 901, provided we have not listed them before. When the list consists of 60 figures, the sample can be identified as the corresponding firms.

5. *How many units should be included in the sample* (and possibly in the various subdivisions of the sample if the sampling design calls for subdividing the sample)? This is a question of *sample size*.[1] In our example of simple random sampling, the question is simply whether n should be 60, as arbitrarily assumed so far, or some other figure. Such important questions will be discussed in some detail later. From a pure statistical point of view, it is always beneficial to have a large sample. The larger the sample, however, the higher the costs.

6. *How should the data be stored and analyzed?* This should be decided before the data are collected. The immediate purpose of a sample survey is often to obtain a table with rows and columns, called a *data matrix* (sample data matrix). An example is shown in Table 7.1.

In this table the *row headings are firms* (units) and the *column headings are variables*, while the *values* of the two variables for the various firms make up the main body of the table. In other words, listed in the left margin of the table are the units, or unit numbers. At the top of the table, the variables are listed. Each horizontal row thus refers to a unit, while each vertical column refers to a variable. This table is commonly stored in a *data file* in a computer. Notice that such a data matrix gives a useful overview of the data regardless of whether the data are primary or secondary, and regardless of the method of collection. Granted that the data have, or can be given, a structure such that the data matrix applies, this form of storing the data should be used, at least initially. The data matrix is the basis for computations leading to parameter estimates, confidence intervals, etc.

Sometimes the intention is to use the sample data matrix as a basis for *further analyses*, like a regression analysis, a discriminant analysis or a factor analysis. In such cases, it is often preferable that the data matrix be relatively simple, and a plain sampling design like simple random sampling should typically be used. In Table 7.1, for instance, we could be interested in regressing R & D expenditures on profits.

> Most data can be conveniently stored in a file where each variable occupies a column, and each unit occupies a row.

An *advantage* of simple random sampling is that the method is easy to understand and apply. The following *drawbacks* can be mentioned:

- A complete frame (a list of all the units in the whole population) is needed.
- The costs of obtaining the sample can be high if the units are geographically widely scattered.
- The *standard errors*[2] of the estimators will typically be large, i.e. the confidence intervals will be wide.

If the units have quite different values for a variable of interest, simple random sampling can be improved by making the probability of inclusion in the sample proportional to the value of the variable. This is called *sampling with probabilities proportional to size*. Thus, if the units are industrial plants and we want to estimate total consumption of toilet paper in the population of plants, we can make the probability that a given plant will be included in the sample proportional to the number of workers in the plant. This should work well since consumption of toilet paper is highly correlated with the number of workers. For further details, see Churchill (1991: 574−6). We will now briefly mention some other sampling designs.

7.4 Stratified random sampling

Suppose we want to estimate the average height of the trees in a forest consisting of three stands denoted by (1), (2) and (3). In stand (1) all trees were cut down 100 years ago, in stand (2) all trees were cut down 15 years ago, and in stand (3) some trees were cut down at various times in the past. All the trees are therefore of about the same age within stand (1) and within stand (2), while the trees within stand (3) are of very different ages. The heights of the trees will, of course, be highly correlated with their ages.

If we take a simple random sample from the population, we may have bad luck and get most of our sample from either stand (1) or stand (2). In both cases the result would probably be quite misleading, assuming that the stands are of comparable size. In cases like this, it is important that the sample be spread throughout the whole population. However, since the trees are very uniform within both stand (1) and stand (2), even a single tree from each of these stands would provide lots of information. Most of the trees in the combined sample should therefore be allocated to stand (3) where the *variance* of the heights of the trees is *largest*.

A *stratum* (plural, strata) is simply a part or subdivision of the population. The *stands* in the forest example are natural strata. A *stratified random sample* is obtained by taking a simple random sample from each stratum. The idea of stratified sampling is to ensure that every part of the population, i.e. every stratum, gets a better representation. This is especially important if the means (or proportions or whatever we want to estimate) are very different in the different strata, as is the case with the mean heights of the trees in our example. The result will be a smaller sampling variation, i.e. more stable results in repeated samples than we would get by using simple random sampling.

Proportional allocation means that the proportion of units included in the sample is the same for each stratum. This principle is simple to apply and often satisfactory. In the forest example, it would be better to take relatively few units from strata (1) and (2) where the variances of the heights are small, and many trees from stratum (3) where the variance of the heights is large. It is also possible to take into account the costs of getting observations and to take few units from the strata where the costs are high — for instance, because of travelling costs.

Usually, a population can be divided into strata in several alternative ways. When applying stratification, it is important to stratify in a fashion that makes the means (or other parameters) rather different in different strata. The more different, the better. Stratified random sampling, like other sophisticated sampling designs, is usually compared to simple random sampling which forms a kind of standard.

Advantages: Stratified random sampling can give higher precision with the same sample size or, alternatively, the same precision with a smaller sample. Stratified sampling can also give separate results for each stratum. Stratified sampling simplifies data collection.

Drawbacks: A complete frame is needed. Depending on the allocation principle applied, additional information like knowledge of standard deviations and costs may be needed for each stratum.

If the population can be divided into strata which are homogeneous within but heterogeneous between, precision can be increased or costs lowered.

7.5   Systematic sampling

A prerequisite for applying systematic sampling is that the units in the population can be ordered in some way. Examples are as follows:

- Records that are ordered in a file.
- Names that are ordered alphabetically in a telephone directory.
- Houses that are ordered along a road.
- Customers who walk one by one through an entrance, and so on.

Thus, the units in the population can be numbered from number 1 (the first unit) up to unit number N (the last unit).

A 10 per cent *systematic sample* is obtained by drawing every tenth unit in the ordered population. Usually the starting unit is determined by drawing at random one of the first ten units in the population. If we use a percentage other than 10, the procedure is similar.

Advantages: The method is simple, but probably the most important advantage is that a frame is not always needed. The method can therefore be used, for instance, to interview a sample of persons passing by a corner during a particular day. The units in the sample will be spread evenly over the ordered population. Sometimes this will increase precision.

Drawbacks: The most important potential drawback is the danger of hidden periodicities. To take an extreme example for illustration, suppose articles produced by a particular machine are sampled systematically with a 10 per cent sample. Suppose further that for some technical reason (a rotating chipped wheel) every tenth article is defective. If one happens to get an unfortunate starting point, the whole sample could consist of defective articles!

7.6 Cluster sampling

A *cluster sample* is a sample where the units making up the population and sample are called clusters. Other names for clusters are first-stage units and primary sampling units. A cluster consists of a collection of more basic, smaller units called second-stage units or secondary sampling units. An example of cluster sampling could be the following. Instead of taking a random sample of workers (second-stage units), one could take a random sample of plants (first-stage units). The workers in a particular plant would then make up a cluster of workers. In *one-stage cluster sampling*, all the workers in the selected plants would be examined.

In *two-stage cluster sampling*, a random sample of plants is first taken, and then a random sample of workers is drawn from each selected plant. Cluster sampling is often used in market research when interviewing household units. Often city blocks are used as clusters. These clusters are constructed on the basis of city maps and the method is often called *area sampling*.

The difference between stratified random sampling and cluster sampling may be a little confusing. Suppose we divide a population into strata and take *a random sample of strata*. In this case we would actually be performing cluster sampling, using the strata as clusters. The crucial difference between the two methods is whether we take a random sample of units *within* each stratum (cluster) as we do in stratified random sampling, or whether we take a random sample of clusters (strata) as we do in cluster sampling. Notice also that in stratified sampling we want the strata to be as different as possible. In cluster sampling the situation is the opposite in that we want the clusters to be as similar as possible.

Systematic sampling can be considered a particular type of cluster sampling where, for instance, units number 1, 11, 21, 31, ..., form one cluster, while units number 2, 12, 22, 32, ..., form the second cluster, and units number 10, 20, 30, 40, ..., form the tenth cluster in a 10 per cent systematic sample. If the random starting point happens to be 6, the cluster (or systematic sample) consisting of units number 6, 16, 26, 36 and so on will be selected. A systematic sample is thus a cluster sample consisting of only one cluster.

Advantages: The major advantage of cluster sampling is that we do not need a complete frame of the secondary sampling units. We do need a frame of the clusters, however. Another important advantage in many kinds of cluster sampling like area sampling is the geographical concentration of the units to be interviewed.

Drawbacks: If there is large variation between clusters in the variables to be examined, the method may yield poor precision.

7.7   Determining sample size

Increased sample size will, in general, improve the quality of the statistical results. If the purpose of the survey is to estimate an unknown parameter, the quality of the result is inversely related to the size of the error of estimation. *The error of estimation* is equal to the absolute value of the difference between the unknown parameter and the estimate. But since the parameter is unknown, the error of estimation also remains unknown. Thus a probability statement is needed.

The quality of the result is often expressed in terms of the precision of the estimator of the unknown parameter. This precision can again be expressed by means of the width of the confidence interval or, equivalently, by means of one-half of this width. This half of the width will decrease when the sample size increases, and it can typically be interpreted in the following way. Suppose the confidence probability is 0.95. Then there is a probability of 0.95 that the error of estimation is, at most, equal to half the width of the confidence interval.

The determination of sample size is important both from a statistical and from an economic point of view. A large sample is almost always better than a small one from a statistical point of view, and is almost always more expensive as well. Thus the starting point for the determination is not necessarily given. The question is, should we start by setting a budget limit or should we start by setting a limit or bound on the error of estimation? The necessary sample size will also depend on the research design or, more specifically, on the sample design, and various designs will induce different costs. In addition, some designs will produce desirable by-products, like results for subdivisions of the population.

Another important fact is that the necessary sample size will also depend on the variability in the population. This variability is measured by a standard deviation. As a matter of fact, this standard deviation is typically unknown and must be assessed before the study is undertaken, possibly by means of a pilot study. A final, important complication is that often not one but several unknown parameters are being estimated in the same sample survey. The necessary sample size may show up to be different for the different parameters. Thus a compromise is necessary.

Example

Suppose that, in our previous example, we want to determine the necessary sample size to estimate the total amount of money budgeted for R & D next year by the whole industry. Formula (7.1) below shows how this can be done. For simplicity, assume we know that there are $N = 1000$ firms in the industry. Suppose further that in a pilot study of ten firms, the minimum and maximum amounts budgeted for R & D were 0 and 1200 money units respectively. Then the range is 1200. If we make the very crude assumption that the range is four times the standard deviation, an estimate of σ is given by $1200 \div 4 = 300$.[3] Suppose further that we want the error of estimation to be at most $E = 25\,000$ money units with a probability of $1 - \alpha = 0.95$. Then we must use the upper 2.5 per cent fractile from the normal distribution which is $Z_{\alpha/2} = 1.96$. Substituting these values into the formula below, we find that necessary sample size is about $n = 357$ firms. Notice that this is just a crude estimate.

$$n = \frac{N\sigma^2}{\dfrac{(N-1)E^2}{Z_{\alpha/2}^2 N^2} + \sigma^2} = \frac{(1000)\,300^2}{\dfrac{(1000-1)\,25\,000^2}{(1.96^2)\,1000^2} + 300^2} = 356.39 \approx 357 \tag{7.1}$$

Similar formulae are available for determining sample size when estimating other kinds of parameter or using other sampling methods (see Scheaffer *et al.*, 1990).

In summary, it is important to be aware of the fact that there is no such thing as a 'correct' sample size. Students doing their first research often seem to be bewildered by this. As a researcher, you should be aware that you and you alone have to make several important decisions. A statistician may guide you, but the choices are all yours.

It is worth noting that the gains in precision from increasing the sample size are large when the sample size is small, and small when the sample size is large. Thus there is a tendency for an optimal sample size. The true optimum will, of course, depend on the choices described earlier, but typically the gains from increasing the sample size to more than, say, 1500 or 2000 are relatively small.

On the other hand, there is usually very much to gain in precision by increasing the sample size up to, say, 400. If you end up with a sample size in the interval from 400 to 1500, your choice is probably not a bad one.

There is no lower limit to the size of a sample that can be useful. A sample of, say, 100 can often give interesting and valuable results. A regression analysis based upon 10–15 observations is often very useful. In everyday life, people continually draw

Sample size is influenced by desired precision and judgements regarding standard deviations.

Table 7.2 Typical sample sizes for studies of human and institutional populations

Number of subgroup analyses	People or households		Institutions	
	National	Regional or special	National	Regional or special
None or few	1000–1500	200–500	200–500	50–200
Average	1500–2500	500–1000	500–1000	200–500
Many	2500+	1000+	1000+	500+

Source: Sudman (1976: 87)

inferences based on a sample size of one or two, a practice which needs to be improved, however.

We should always remember that results from probability samples are uncertain, but that the reliability of such results can be calculated and will improve with the sample size. Sudman (1976: 87) gives a table showing typical sample sizes that have been used in various kinds of investigation (Table 7.2).

A serious potential threat to the validity of results from sampling surveys is *non-response*. When some units which have been drawn for inclusion in the sample do not respond to our questions, the effective *sample size is reduced*. But this is not the main problem, since it can easily be remedied. Thus, if we need a sample of 400 units and we expect a 50 per cent response rate, we could take a sample of 800 units to counteract the non-response.

The real problem with non-response is that *those who do not respond are usually different from those who do respond*. To take an extreme example, suppose we use a mail questionnaire to learn something about consumption patterns for alcoholic beverages. The majority of the real drinkers will probably not respond for several reasons, but they make up an important part of the whole picture. Therefore, it is very important to get responses also from the drinkers who have been picked out by our sampling procedure. For further details regarding how to deal with the problem of non-response, see Churchill (1991: 614–28).

Notes

1. In *stratified sampling* we also need to determine how the total sample should be allocated between the strata. *Cluster sampling* requires definition of clusters.
2. The (estimated) standard deviation of an estimator, i.e. the square root of its (estimated) variance, is often called its *standard error*. (For further discussion, see Cochran, 1977: 25.)
3. Of course, we would typically use the ten observations from the pilot study to compute the sample standard deviation s and use this as an estimate of σ. But we wanted to explain a method which can be useful if we just make a judgement about the range without having any data.

CHAPTER 8

Qualitative methods

Alternatives to the standard approach, like unstructured interviewing, tend to be viewed as faulted variants . . . I am arguing, instead, that the standard survey interview is itself essentially faulted and that it therefore cannot serve as the ideal ideological model against which to assess other approaches.

(Mishler, 1986: 29)

In the literature on research methods, there is some discussion on which methods or techniques are more suitable or 'scientific'. It is sometimes stated that structured and quantitative methods are more 'scientific' and thereby better. But in our opinion, methods or techniques are not 'better' or 'scientific' only because they are quantitative. As mentioned earlier, which methods and techniques are most suitable for which research (project) depends on the research problem and its purpose (Jankowicz, 1991).

Research methods refer to the systematic, focused and orderly collection of data for the purpose of obtaining information from it, to solve/answer our research problems or questions. The methods are different from the techniques of data collection. By methods we mean data collection through historical review and analysis, surveys, field experiments and case studies, while by techniques we mean a step-by-step procedure that we follow to gather data and analyze them for finding the answers to our research questions. These are concerned more with how to do things than with what to do or why to do it. In business studies, we normally use techniques such as structured, semi-structured or unstructured interviews, surveys and observations (Bennett, 1986; Jankowicz, 1991).

The main difference between qualitative and quantitative research is not 'quality' but procedure. In qualitative research, findings are not arrived at by statistical methods or other procedures of quantification. The difference between quantitative and qualitative methods is not just a question of quantification, but also a reflection of different

83

QUALITATIVE METHODS	QUANTITATIVE METHODS
• Emphasis on understanding	• Emphasis on testing and verification
• Focus on understanding from respondent's/informant's point of view	• Focus on facts and/or reasons of social events
• Interpretation and rational approach	• Logical and critical approach
• Observations and measurements in natural settings	• Controlled measurement
• Subjective 'insider view' and closeness to data	• Objective 'outsider view' distant from data
• Explorative orientation	• Hypothetical-deductive; focus on hypothesis testing
• Process oriented	• Result oriented
• Holistic perspective	• Particularistic and analytical
• Generalization by comparison of properties and contexts of individual organism	• Generalization by population membership

Source: Based on Reichardt and Cook (1979).

Figure 8.1 The difference in emphasis in qualitative versus quantitative methods

perspectives on knowledge and research objectives. We can do research on behaviour, events, organizational functioning, social environments, interaction and relationships. In some of these studies, data may be quantified, but the analysis itself is qualitative, such as with census reports. It is quite common for researchers to collect their data through observations and interviews, the methods normally related to qualitative research. But the research may code the data collected in such a manner that it would allow statistical analysis. In other words, it is quite possible to quantify qualitative data. Qualitative and quantitative methods are therefore not mutually exclusive. The difference is in the overall form and in the emphasis and objectives of the study.

Qualitative research is a mixture of the rational, explorative and intuitive, where the skills and experience of the researcher play an important role in the analysis of data. Qualitative research is often focused on social process and not on social structures, which is often the case in quantitative research. The skills needed to do qualitative research are: thinking abstractly, stepping back and critically analyzing situations, recognizing and avoiding biases, obtaining valid and reliable information, having theoretical and social sensitivity and the ability to keep analytical distance while at the same time utilizing past experience, and a shrewd sense of observation and interaction (van Maanen, 1983; Strauss and Corbin, 1990). Although most researchers emphasize one or the other, qualitative and quantitative methods can be combined and used in the same study. The differences in the emphasis between qualitative and quantitative methods are illustrated in Figure 8.1.

8.1 When to use qualitative methods

As mentioned earlier, the main reasons for doing qualitative research and using qualitative methods are the objective of the research project and the background and previous experience of the researcher. Some disciplines, such as anthropology, or philosophical orientations, such as phenomenology, particularly advocate qualitative methods for data collection and data analysis. For our purpose, however, the main reason should be the research problem and the focus and objectives of the study.

Research problems focusing on uncovering a person's experience or behaviour, or where we want to uncover and understand a phenomenon about which little is known, are typical examples of problems requiring qualitative research. Moreover, when an event or a social process is difficult to study with quantitative methods, qualitative methods are most suitable and can provide intricate details and understanding. Qualitative research is thus common in social and behavioural sciences, and among practitioners who want to understand human behaviour and functions. It is quite suitable for studying organizations, groups and individuals (Strauss and Corbin, 1990).

There are three major components of qualitative research (Becker, 1970; Miles and Huberman, 1984; Strauss and Corbin, 1990):

1. Data: often collected through interviews and observations.
2. Interpretive or analytical procedure: the techniques to conceptualize and analyze the data to arrive at findings or theories.
3. Report: written or verbal. In the case of students, the report is written in the form of a thesis or project.

One argument for using quantitative data is that quite often we collect individual data and aggregate them to analyze organizations. To separate pre-decided elements we use pre-developed instruments and analyze the results quantitatively. In this manner we can only get a limited reality because pre-developed instruments may not suit the particular situation, and also because these methods cut reality into discrete pieces which are then combined into statistical clusters (for more details, see, for example, Glaser and Strauss, 1967; Weiss, 1968; Light, 1979; van Maanen, 1983; Eisenhardt, 1989).

In spite of the claim by the above authors that relatively few studies use qualitative methods, it is not difficult to find support for the usage of qualitative data:

> Qualitative data are attractive for many reasons. They are rich, full, earthly, holistic, real; their face validity seems unimpeachable, they preserve chronological flow where that is important, and suffer minimally from retrospective distortion; and they, in principle, offer a far more precise way to assess causality in organizational affairs than arcane efforts like cross-lagged correlations. (Miles, 1979: 117)

It is generally accepted that, for inductive and exploratory research, qualitative methods are most useful, as they can lead us to hypothesis building and explanations. According to this view, qualitative and quantitative methods are suitable at different stages or levels of research. At the first level, the problem is of an unstructured nature and qualitative methods are suitable. At the second level, quantitative methods are most useful, as here we want to test different hypotheses which were arrived at through level one. Quantitative methods allow us to accept or reject these hypotheses in a logical and consistent manner. At the third level, both qualitative and quantitative methods can be used. Often a combination of the two methods is used at this level. The combined method is called 'multi-method' or 'triangulation' (triangulation is treated separately in this chapter).

8.2 Types of qualitative method

Qualitative methods, as defined earlier in this section, are flexible and unstructured. As compared to quantitative methods, they employ a limited number of observations and try to explain different aspects of our problem area. Although the number of observations is low, several aspects of the problem area can be analyzed. Low numbers are also justified because we often want to do in-depth studies or provide 'thick description' which is not possible in cases of numerous observations. Qualitative methods are, therefore, most suitable when the objectives of the study demand in-depth insight into a phenomenon.

Different qualitative methods are suitable for different types of study. We have also stated in the earlier pages that quite often we can combine qualitative and quantitative methods. Many scholars claim that the two approaches are complementary and cannot be used in isolation from each other. (For this type of discussion, see Jones, 1988; Martin, 1988; Jankowicz, 1991.) According to this view, no *method* is entirely qualitative or quantitative. However, the *techniques* can be either quantitative or qualitative. Figure 8.2 illustrates this point further.

As we can see in Figure 8.2, the methods from left to right become more quantitative and use more quantitative techniques. Historical review, group discussions and case studies are mostly qualitative research methods. These qualitative methods use relatively more qualitative techniques, such as conversation and in-depth semi-structured interviews.

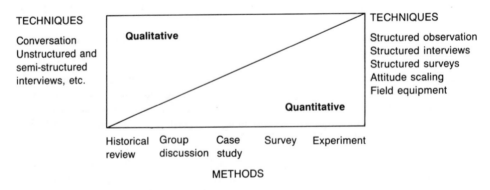

Source: Based on Jankowicz (1991: 159).

Figure 8.2 Qualitative and quantitative methods and techniques

8.2.1 Historical review

In the case of historical reviews, our job is to describe what happened in the past so that we can understand the present or plan for the future. Here we go through existing records and reports, and talk to different people to get as true a picture as possible. The archives are reviewed with a rather interrogative manner and with a particular research question/ problem in mind. The main problem with using such a method is that we have to trust human memory, which records selective parts of our reality. It is quite possible that two different people, while going through a certain situation or experience, will record or remember different things; sometimes they make mistakes or misunderstand. It is therefore important that, while using such a method, we should cross-check one written source with another, or a written source with an interview, or two interviews with each other. In other words, we have to be critical and compare different explanations for the situation or event. For further insight into historical reviews as a research method, we recommend Orbell (1987).

8.2.2 Group discussion

The second qualitative method mentioned above is group discussions (also referred to as focus groups). In this type of research method, the researcher can get together with several respondents at the same time and initiate a discussion on a certain topic. The opinions of the respondents are considered as information and analyzed later on. This method differs from other methods such as in-depth interviews in the sense that here the interaction is not only between the interviewer and the respondent, but also among the respondents. It is also considered as a relatively cheap and convenient way of gathering information from several respondents in a short time.

Here we should be aware of the influence that the group itself will have on the discussion and information that is exchanged. The discussion is influenced by the size of the group, its composition, the personalities of the people involved, the roles they are asked to play, the physical and geographical arrangement of the meeting, and the 'chemistry' between the interviewer and the group or individuals. It is thus apparent that information gathered by this method will be different from information gathered through historical review and case studies. However, this method is widely used in some research cultures: for example, in the UK this method is so widely used that it is regarded as synonymous with qualitative research (Kent, 1989). In our opinion, however, the case study method (also called in-depth interviews) is becoming extremely popular in business studies. We therefore treat case studies separately and in more detail in the next section.

8.3 Case study method

In relatively less-known areas, where there is little experience and theory available to serve as a guide, intensive study of selected examples is a very useful method of gaining insight and suggesting hypotheses for further research. In our discipline, the case study method is often used for these types of study. The main focus is on seeking insight rather than testing: instead of testing existing hypotheses we seek insight through the features and characteristics of the object being studied. A second feature is the intensity of the study of the object, individual, group, organization, culture, incident or situation. We need to have sufficient information to characterize, to explain the unique features of the case, as well as to point out the characteristics that are common in several cases. Finally, this approach relies on integrative powers of research: the ability to study an object with many dimensions and then to draw an integrative interpretation (Selltiz *et al.*, 1976).

This is a preferred method when 'how' or 'why' questions are to be answered, when the researcher has little control over events and when the focus is on a current phenomenon in a real-life context (Yin, 1989). Thus case studies are often of an explanatory, exploratory or descriptive nature. According to Eisenhardt, case studies are:

> particularly well-suited to new research areas or research areas for which existing theory seems inadequate. This type of work is highly complementary to incremental theory building from normal science research. The former is useful in early stages of research on a topic or when a fresh perspective is needed, while the latter is useful in later stages of knowledge. (1989: 548−9)

According to Yin (1989), when to use which research method depends upon:

- the type of research questions;
- the control of the researcher over behavioural events; and
- the focus on a current as opposed to historical phenomenon.

When research questions concern only 'what' — for example, 'What are the ways in which an effective firm is operated?' — an exploratory study is justified. Here the objective is to develop hypotheses or propositions which can later be studied. For an exploratory study, any of the five research strategies can be used. If the questions relate to 'How many?' or 'How much?', survey or archival strategies are favoured. But when 'how' and 'why' questions are asked, a case study method is favoured as a research strategy.

Quite often it is stated that the case study method is used when we want to study a single organization and want to identify factors involved in some aspect or behaviour of an organization or smaller unit, such as a marketing or finance department. However, it is equally possible to study a number of organizations with regard to a set of variables we have already identified or assumed. Such case studies are called *comparative case studies*. In this type of study, we ask or study the same questions in a number of organizations and compare them with each other to draw conclusions.

The purpose of data collection in the comparative case study method is to compare (replicate) the organizations studied with each other in a systematic way, to explore different dimensions of our research issues or to examine different levels of research variables. In survey, on the other hand, we are more concerned with the sampling of different organizations because we want to generalize our findings to all other organizations of the same type (Jankowicz, 1991). Yin (1984) compares the case study method with experiments and suggests three situations where case study is the preferred method:

- If we want to follow a theory which specifies a particular set of outcomes in some particular situation, and if we find a firm which finds itself in that particular situation, we can use the case study method for a critical test of theory and its applicability to the organization.
- If we want to study some specific characteristics of a rare or extreme situation in which an organization finds itself, we can use the case study method to compare and contrast.
- If we want to study a situation or an organization which has rarely been studied and is unique in its nature, we can use the case study method. In this case, we hope to learn something new and important.

As most case studies are done through a review of existing historical material and records plus interviews, the case study method is quite similar to historical review, but it is different in the sense that here we have a possibility of direct observation and interaction. As mentioned earlier, we would like to make it explicit that the case study method is not synonymous with qualitative research or methods. A case study may very well involve quantitative methods or even be entirely quantitative.

8.3.1 Preparing for a case study

In many cases, especially in business studies, students first decide which method to use — for example, case study or survey — and then formulate their problem. We have been advocating that it is the research problem and the research objectives that should dictate the type of method we use. Here lies a dilemma: should we decide the method first, or should our problem lead us to the method? Of course, the latter should be the case, as most problems and research objectives clearly suggest one form of data collection over another. Once our research problem suggests case study as the preferred data collection method, we should deal with questions such as: what are the skills needed to conduct case study? What types of *a priori* assumption do we have? How do we select the cases? How many cases shall we include in our study? How shall we conduct the case study?

As far as the *skills* required are concerned, case studies are one of the most difficult types of research to do, as they demand special skills from the researcher. Some training for specific cases is necessary, especially if the researcher has no previous experience of conducting case studies or if a research assistant is used with multiple cases. Unlike surveys, where data collection is more routinized, in case studies the researcher has to be skilled in the dynamics of a case and should be able to take advantage of opportunities offered during the data collection.

While collecting data through semi-structured interviews, a researcher must be able to control the situation, ask the right questions, adapt to new or unexpected situations and develop trust. All these skills can be learned if the researcher is aware of them beforehand. Yin (1989: 67) recommends case study training as a seminar experience, especially in multiple cases where several researchers are involved. Moreover, he recommends protocol development by all the researchers individually, followed by a review of each other's protocol to arrive at the final one. One purpose of these seminars and protocols should be to discuss potential problems and how to handle them. Such training may also reveal weaknesses in the research problem, in the study design and even in the capabilities of researchers. All these things can be improved if detected. It is also recommended that before the data collection is started, a pilot study should be conducted. It serves as a rehearsal for the data collection procedures, indicating the time it takes and any problems that may arise.

8.3.2   A priori *propositions*

For exploratory and inductive types of study, we should have research questions such as 'how', 'why' and 'where' clear before we decide on which type of case study design we should have. If the purpose of the study is to explore, we do not need to have propositions. For descriptive or causal studies, we should have a theoretical base and clearly stated propositions (for further discussion, see Eisenhardt, 1989; Yin, 1989; Strauss and Corbin, 1990).

The idea is that there should be a link between data and propositions. Campbell (1975) discusses 'pattern matching', where several pieces of information from one or several cases are related to propositions. If we can find a systematic or unsystematic pattern, we can accept or reject our propositions. In such studies, statistical tests are not necessary to establish a pattern and there are no precise ways of testing or setting criteria for interpreting these findings. The pattern has to be sufficiently systematic to accept certain propositions. The conclusion is that in causal studies, and sometimes also in descriptive studies, theory building prior to data collection is necessary (Yin, 1989: 36).

8.3.3   *How to select the cases*

As in other methods of data collection, it is important to decide the target population which is to be used for the investigation. It includes those firms, individuals, groups or elements that will be represented in the study. The next stage is to assess the accessible population, the population to which we can have access (Cooper, 1984). Out of this accessible population we have to select one or a few cases, objects or firms, for study. The time available for the study, financial resources for travelling and other practical issues are of great importance. For example, depending upon how much time we have to study, the type of organization or company we select for our study will be different. If we have very little time available, we should perhaps study a smaller firm, as in these firms the communication lines are smaller and faster, they are more flexible and it is easier to get overall or in-depth information.

On the other hand, if we are studying a specific and complex issue, we should perhaps study a bigger firm, as these firms experience complex problems and have expertise in-house that can provide us with in-depth information on the particular issue (v.d. Meer-Kooistra, 1993). The cases should also correspond with our theoretical framework and the variables we are studying. For example, if we are studying the behaviour of industrial buyers, we have to select firms that are dealing with industrial marketing and purchasing. Once we have selected a firm, the same goes for the question of whom we should interview. In the above case, it has to be a manager who is involved in the process of marketing and purchasing. An interview with the firm's public relations manager or an accountant would not provide us with the information we were looking for.

In bigger organizations it is very important to select the right department, section or individual. It is a question not of interviewing the most important individuals, but of interviewing the *right person* from an organization: right from the point of view of our research questions and study variables. Finding the right person is sometimes a long process. However, if we are able to establish contact with a key, or highly placed, manager, our goal should be to ask for his help in identifying the right person.

Students often ask how many cases they should include in their study. The answer to this question is very difficult as there is no upper or lower limit to the number of cases to be included in a study. Many times only one case is enough. As Mintzberg says: 'What, for example, is wrong with a sample size of one? Why should researchers have to apologize for them? Should Piaget apologize for studying his own children, a physicist for splitting only one atom?' (1979: 583). It is the research problem and the research objectives that influence the number and choice of cases to be studied. Campbell (1975) argues for richness of detail within a single case by looking for multiple implications of the ideas under study.

8.3.4 How to conduct a case study

Special skills and some caution are required for the case study method. Data collection in a case study design is crucial, as the whole study depends on it. Normally, data collection through case studies is considered an easy method, but this is a misconception. In fact, data collection through case studies is much more demanding than through surveys or experiments. In this method the researcher needs to collect data personally, and the use of mail questionnaires or research assistants is not a recommended strategy. The researcher conducting a case study must be fully aware of and should comprehend the research problem and purpose of the study. S/he should not only be able to ask relevant and probing questions, but should also have the capabilities to listen and interpret the answers given. To understand the received information properly, the researcher has to be very observant and a very good listener. In other words, researchers should be able to read between the lines and understand not only what is said but also what is meant. They must also be careful not to let their biases influence the interpretation. This is particularly important in single case studies, as the researcher has no other case with which to compare the findings.

In the case study method, a researcher can seldom follow a pre-planned procedure or timetable, and often the time, the number of cases to be studied, the scope of cases to be

	Single case designs	Multiple case designs
Holistic (single unit of analysis)	TYPE 1	TYPE 3
Embedded (multiple units of analysis)	TYPE 2	TYPE 4

Source: Yin (1989: 46).

Figure 8.3 Basic designs for case studies

studied, and even the purpose and research questions are subject to modifications and changes. For each change, the researcher has to find new arguments and justifications. At the same time, if the study, research questions and purpose are constantly modified or adapted to new conditions, there is a risk that a gap may arise between the original study planned and the study actually undertaken.

> In the case study approach you have to create a balance between rigour and flexibility.

When several people are involved in collecting data for the same study, or when research assistants are used to collect data through this method, the investigators or assistants need to be trained properly. The risk of a lack of training is also apparent in group work, when two or more students write a thesis together. In this situation, all members of the group should be involved in all parts of the thesis, especially in the earlier stages when problem definition and research design are decided upon. The members should keep each other informed and those who have earlier experience should train other members of the group so that they can conduct case studies efficiently (see also section 6.2 on interviewing).

8.3.5 Different types of case study design

Yin suggests four types of case study design, and presents a 2 × 2 matrix (Figure 8.3) suggesting that single and multiple case studies reflect different design considerations. The four types of research design are as follows:

1. Single case design, holistic.

2. Single case design, embedded.
3. Multiple case design, holistic.
4. Multiple case design, embedded.

As we can see, the primary distinction is between single and multiple case designs. We should therefore decide, at an early stage, whether we are going to use single or multiple case design.

Single case is appropriate when a particular case is a critical case and we want to use it for testing an established theory. It is a critical case because it meets all the conditions necessary to confirm, challenge or extend the theory. Another situation is when a single case is an extreme or a unique case. Finally, a single case design is appropriate when a case is revelatory. This means that we can observe and study a phenomenon which was previously not accessible and which can provide useful insight. We can also use single case design in other situations, such as in a pilot study or as an exploratory study that serves as a first step to a later, more comprehensive study (Yin, 1989: 47−9).

Multiple case study design is considered more appropriate for studies not involving rare, critical or revelatory cases. In this approach we should be clear that every case has to serve a particular purpose in the study. In other words, we have to justify the selection of each case. However, as pointed out earlier, case study design is often flexible and can be changed, modified or revised with proper justification.

The use of a particular case study method depends also upon the type of study we are doing, whether it is inductive or deductive, and also upon whether we are looking for specific or general explanations. In the case of an inductive approach and specific explanation, we may use the single case. On the other hand, if we are doing a study with a deductive approach, we can use the case study at an early stage to develop our hypotheses or propositions. If we are doing a study with an inductive approach, but are looking for general explanations, then we should use a multiple case method. However, if we are doing a study with a deductive approach and are looking for generalizations, then the case study is a less recommended method. We recommend that students using this method should consult Yin (1989) for further guidance.

8.4 Triangulation

Triangulation refers to the combination of methodologies in the study of the same phenomenon. Through triangulation we can improve the accuracy of judgements and results by collecting data through different methods or even collecting different kinds of data on the subject matter of our study. The discussion on validity in Chapter 5 is particularly relevant here. Sometimes to enhance the validity of our research, we need to collect or analyze data through triangulation. In cases where correctness or precision is important, it is quite logical to collect information through different methods and angles. The following story illustrates what we mean.

Three blind men were asked to describe an elephant by touching or feeling only a part of it. We can well imagine what they could have described by touching different parts of

an elephant such as a foot, an ear or a trunk. This illustrates that, in many cases, a single method will not be enough to explain or describe a phenomenon, and that we need to use a multi-method approach to get the whole reality.

The use of multi-methods or triangulation is not new and can be traced back to Campbell and Fiske (1959), who argued that to ensure validation one should use more than one method. The main advantage of triangulation, however, is that it can produce a more complete, holistic and contextual portrait of the object under study. Moreover, it is quite useful to use qualitative methods in a pilot study to build hypotheses or propositions, and then to use quantitative methods to test these hypotheses. We can call this a two-step study.

There are some problems with triangulation. For example, sometimes it can be difficult to judge if the results from different methods are consistent or not. A second problem arises when the different methods come up with contradictory results. Sometimes researchers prefer or emphasize one method over another: for example, quantitative versus qualitative approaches. However, all research methods have advantages and disadvantages when it comes to different research problems. Our conclusion is that triangulation or the use of a multi-method approach on the same study object can be useful even if we do not get the same results. It can lead us to a better understanding or to new questions that can be answered by later research.

Table 8.1 Methods of data collection to study managerial issues

Method	Major advantage(s)	Major disadvantage(s)
Secondary sources	Convenient; draws analyses from others	Data frequently unavailable, inappropriate or incomplete
Questionnaire and interview	Convenient	Data of questionable reliability
Unstructured observation	Enables researcher to understand new dimensions and to probe	Non-systematic (may lose important data, cannot replicate); inefficient
Structured observation	Enables researcher to understand new dimensions, to probe, to be systematic	Inefficient (consumes much researcher time); difficult to interpret some activities
Activity sampling	Efficient; recording by researcher	Little help in developing understanding of new dimensions; non-continuous, hence interpretation difficult

Source: Based on Mintzberg (1973: 229).

Mintzberg (1973), after reviewing research on management issues, distinguished seven research methods. We summarize his views in Table 8.1, but only for those methods which we have previously described.

8.5 Analyzing qualitative data

We can collect qualitative as well as quantitative data through qualitative methods. Generally we refer to data as quantitative when they are statistically analyzed and are expressed, presented or measured in numbers. Data which cannot be statistically analyzed and are difficult to measure in numbers are often called qualitative: for example, strong, weak, easy or difficult. One main problem in analyzing qualitative data is that, on one hand, the number of observations is so low and, on the other hand, the information on the case or cases is so in-depth that it is very easy for the researcher to be drawn into the sheer volume of cases. It is often difficult for students to filter or discard irrelevant data before analysis. With qualitative methods the analysis is also difficult because data collection and analysis are often done simultaneously, and sometimes the research

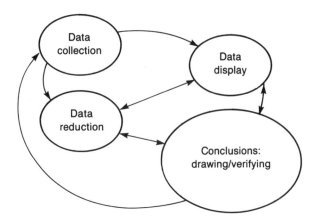

Source: Miles and Huberman (1984: 23).

Figure 8.4 Components of data analysis: interactive model

problem is even formulated or reformulated at the same time. This often leads to new questions and new data collection, and there is no definite phase of data analysis (Grønhaug, 1985). Figure 8.4 illustrates this process.

To analyze data we have to code them so that they can be broken down, conceptualized, put together and presented in an understandable manner. As qualitative studies quite often help in building theories, coding requires extra care, and a balance between creativity, rigour and persistence has to be achieved. We should, however, remember that data collection and data analysis are closely interconnected, and while collecting data we should have already considered data analysis, as this will have influenced our sampling and coding procedure as well as what type of data was to be collected.

In social sciences and especially in business studies, we have two viewpoints. One suggests that, in principle, all data can be classified and measured. In this case, all data collected through qualitative methods should be coded and refined in such a way that it allows categorization and quantification. This attitude is often referred to as the *positivistic orientation*. On the other hand, the second viewpoint suggests that individual cases are meaningful in their own right and that it is not necessary to have data that allow categorization and quantification on some kind of scale. This orientation is often referred to as the *phenomenological attitude*. Our purpose here is not to discuss these two orientations and recommend one or the other, as both attitudes are found in research and business studies. However, while using qualitative methods, it is more common for researchers to follow the phenomenological approach, that each case or observation may depict and point out its uniqueness. Our opinion is that qualitative data can be used in analysis and interpretation, irrespective of whether they have been quantified or not. This type of data, as mentioned earlier, provides new integrative insights due to an understanding of a phenomenon.

CHAPTER 9

Data analysis

Teach us to count our days that we learn to be wise.

(Psalms 90.12)

The purpose of this chapter is to give simple demonstrations of how to analyze data. It is assumed that the reader has been through a basic course in business statistics. More details regarding statistical reasoning and formulae are given in Appendix A for those who do not have the necessary background or who need a refreshment. Sometimes the researcher can be overwhelmed by a large 'bunch of data', however, if you have followed the guidelines of the previous chapters, you will *know* the purpose of data collection. You should carefully study the principles of research outlined in previous chapters and the examples of data analysis described here *before* you start working with actual data. If you have already collected your data, it may actually be too late to read this chapter!

> Define the problem and choose the method of analysis. *Then* collect and analyze the data.

9.1 Coding and storing your observations

Most likely, you will want to get your data into a data file so that you can analyze them on a computer. You can save enormous amounts of work and frustration if you plan this in detail before you get involved with actual data. Of course, this is difficult, but you should try to foresee, as far as possible, what you may possibly want to do with your data, what kinds of computer program will be used and what kinds of difficulty may emerge in terms of unexpected categories, refusal to answer certain questions, etc.

You should take into account that the data ought to be scrutinized for errors and outliers at some stage. Granted all this, you will often save time and resources by making the flow of data from the source to the computer as short as possible. Depending on the situation, you may find it useful to have more than one data file, but typically you will have one major file where each column corresponds to a variable and each row corresponds to a unit or an individual. The total collection of columns in a file will be referred to as the *data matrix*.[1]

Coding means defining categories and assigning a number to each category. Coding is usually necessary for non-numerical variables, and often each value is given a code, i.e. a number. Numerical variables may also be categorized and coded, but then information is lost, since individual observations are grouped into classes represented by intervals. You should therefore use the original values of numerical variables rather than coding, unless you have a good reason for coding. Coding of numerical variables can always be done at a later stage of the research if you find it useful. Some methods of analysis require data in a certain form. If you code your data before you know the methods of analysis, you may exclude certain methods, like regression analysis, where observed values of each variable are needed for each unit.

Let us take the following examples. For the variable 'sex', the value 'male' could be coded as '1' and the value 'female' could be coded as '2'. Irregular responses could be coded as 'No information' = '8', 'Don't know' = '9' and 'Does not apply' = '0', while the regular responses to the question are coded as '1', '2', '3', etc. When you have scrutinized your data and arrived at the analysis stage, you will typically use the computer to replace these irregular responses by the missing value code of your data program. In the statistical package Minitab, for instance, the missing value code is ' * '. Rows where one or more ' * 's occur will automatically be omitted from certain computations like regression analyses. Variables with values on, for instance, a seven-point scale, where '1' = 'Strongly disagree' and '7' = 'Strongly agree', need no further coding, but can be entered like numerical variables into the data file.

If we allow a single question to be answered with more than one answer simultaneously by a single respondent (multiple response), special care should be exercised in the data matrix. One variable should then be created for each possible response, i.e. each piece of information should get a separate column. For example, we might ask the following question of people who have bought a bicycle: 'Why did you buy a bicycle?' Suppose further that we provide the following alternative answers: (1) to use it to get to my job/school. (2) Because it is healthy to use it. (3) Other reasons. Then we should use three columns (variables) in the data matrix corresponding to the three alternatives. A respondent marking the first two alternatives will then get a '1' in the column corresponding to (1), a '1' in the column corresponding to (2) and a '0' in the column corresponding to (3).

> Make up a detailed plan of what to do with the data before you code them and put them into data files.

9.2   The use of statistical software packages

Using statistical methods today generally means applying a statistical computer program. Many excellent statistical packages are available both for mainframe and for personal computers. Among the widely used packages are SPSS, SAS, Minitab and many others. Unless you are an advanced user or have very special needs, which is unlikely, it does not matter much which package you are using. At least at the elementary and intermediate level, most of the commonly used packages produce comparable print-outs and, if we show you how to interpret print-outs from one package, you will also be able to deal with print-outs from other packages. In order to be concrete in our recommendations, we will show actual print-outs in the following, and we have chosen to use Minitab throughout. Minitab is widely available and easy to use, but you can just as easily use another package. Many packages are now available for Windows or for the Macintosh, and are thus very easy to use. Packages like SAS and SPSS are in certain respects more powerful than Minitab.

Notice that the manuals of the major packages contain very useful guidance for the use of various methods. In addition, they help you find relevant literature. See especially SAS Institute Inc. (1988), but also Norušis/SPSS Inc. (1990) and Minitab Inc. (1993).

9.3   Analyzing one variable

Analysis is often based upon some sort of 'classification' and 'comparison'. Suppose, for instance, that we are interested in car ownership per household in a certain population of households. Each household can then be classified according to the number of cars owned. The observations in a random sample of $n = 100$ households could be classified in a *univariate frequency distribution*, as shown in Table 9.1.

Table 9.1   Car ownership per household in a random sample

x = Number of cars owned	h = absolute frequency = number of households	h/n = relative frequency	Percentage
0	3	0.03	3
1	45	0.45	45
2	37	0.37	37
3	11	0.11	11
4	4	0.04	4
Total	100	1.00	100

```
Histogram of Cars    N = 100

Midpoint  Count
    0       3    ***
    1      45    *********************************************************
    2      37    *************************************************
    3      11    ***********
    4       4    ****
```

Figure 9.1 Histogram of the data in Table 9.1

Here each number of cars forms a class or category. Intervals can also be used: for instance, 0, 1−2 and 3−4 cars. In general, the categories should be *exhaustive* and *mutually exclusive*. This means that any household can be assigned to one and only one category, i.e. the classification should be complete and non-overlapping. Figure 9.1 shows a simple computer-produced histogram (and frequency table) for the data in Table 9.1.

The data in Table 9.1 can also be described by means of various sample measures. From the histogram, we see immediately that the mode (sample mode) is 1 car. Using a computer, we can get the *mean, median, standard deviation* (STDEV), *minimum* (MIN), *maximum* (MAX), *first quartile* (Q1), *third quartile* (Q3), etc., as shown below:

	N	MEAN	MEDIAN	STDEV
Cars	100	1.6800	2.0000	0.8632

	MIN	MAX	Q1	Q3
Cars	0.0000	4.0000	1.0000	2.0000

Table 9.1 is a bare description of a variable in a sample. But such a table contains data for just a (relatively small) sample from the whole population. Can we be sure that the tendency found in this table is true for the whole population? This is the kind of question we ask in our research work.

> In research, we are interested not in the sample, but in the population.

In connection with Table 9.1, the mean number of cars per household in the whole population would typically be denoted by μ and referred to as an *unknown population mean*. The corresponding sample mean, $\bar{x} = 1.68$, is an estimate (point estimate) of μ and will typically be used instead of μ for all practical purposes. Assuming that the number of cars per household is normally distributed, *95 per cent confidence limits* for μ can be obtained, utilizing the Student's *t*-distribution. The result is shown below:

	N	MEAN	STDEV	95.0 PER CENT C.I.
Cars	100	1.6800	0.8632	(1.5087, 1.8513)

We see that the number of observations is 100, the sample mean, $\bar{x}$, is 1.68, the sample standard deviation, s, is 0.8632, the lower confidence limit of μ is 1.5087 and the upper confidence limit of μ is 1.8513. We have chosen to use the confidence probability $1 - \alpha = 0.95$. Thus, we may conclude that the best guess on μ is 1.68 cars per household. Further, there is a probability of 0.95 that the two confidence limits 1.51 and 1.85 have happened to fall such that the interval between them contains the true μ-value.

An alternative to using this t-based method is to use a non-parametric method. Computer output showing results from computing a *Wilcoxon confidence interval* for the population median is given below (Minitab Inc., 1993: 18−7):

	N	ESTIMATED MEDIAN	ACHIEVED CONFIDENCE	CONFIDENCE INTERVAL
Cars	100	1.500	95.0	(1.500, 2.000)

This method is preferable if the population is not normal, and it competes well with the t-method also if the normality assumption is fulfilled.

Suppose we want to test the hypothesis, H: $\mu = 1.55$ cars per household. The reason for using the hypothetical value 1.55 could be that this figure is known to be true in a similar population. If we have no further prior knowledge, we will typically use a two-sided alternative to H, namely A: $\mu \neq 1.55$. Suppose, in addition, that we choose to use a level of significance $\alpha = 0.05$ which *corresponds* to our confidence probability (0.95 + 0.05 = 1). Then we could use the confidence interval to test the hypothesis. Since the hypothetical value, 1.55, is inside the confidence interval, the hypothesis cannot be rejected. In general, if we use a two-sided alternative, and if α corresponds to $1 - \alpha$, we reject H if the hypothetical value is found to be outside the confidence interval.

Before we looked at the data, we might have obtained some knowledge which assures that μ cannot possibly be smaller than 1.55 (somewhat artificial in this particular example). Then our alternative would be A: $\mu > 1.55$. Assuming, as before, that the number of cars per household is normally distributed, a Student's t-test would result in the following output:

TEST OF MU = 1.5500 VERSUS MU GREATER THAN 1.5500

	N	MEAN	STDEV	SE MEAN	T	P-VALUE
Cars	100	1.6800	0.8632	0.0863	1.51	0.068

Since we have used a one-sided alternative, we are now closer to rejection. But still the hypothesis cannot be rejected, since the test statistic 1.51 is smaller than the critical value. We do not have to look up the critical value in a t-table, since the P-value 0.068 has been computed. This value is larger than the level of significance 0.05 which we have chosen. Thus the hypothesis H cannot be rejected.

Finally, let us suppose that for some reason we want to test the hypothesis, H, that 5 per cent of the households in the population have 0 cars per household, 40 per cent have 1 car, 40 per cent have 2 cars, 10 per cent have 3 cars and 5 per cent have 4 cars. The alternative hypothesis, A, is that not all the percentages or probabilities above are true.

The hypothesis can be tested using a chi-square test. This test is often called the test of *goodness of fit*. The test statistic χ_H^2 is based upon the observed frequencies O_i for the various numbers of cars and the corresponding estimated expected frequencies E_i. The formula for the test statistic and the computed value is given below, together with the number of degrees of freedom, which is equal to the number of categories minus one:

$$\chi_H^2 = \sum_{i=1}^{k} \frac{(O_i - E_i)^2}{E_i} = 1.950$$

$$d.f. = k - 1 = 5 - 1 = 4$$

(9.1)

If H is true, the chi-square statistic follows the chi-square distribution with $5 - 1 = 4$ degrees of freedom, since there are $k = 5$ categories in the problem. If we choose the level of significance 0.05, the critical value found in a fractile table of the chi-square distribution is 9.488. Since 1.95 is not greater than 9.488, the conclusion is that H *cannot be rejected* at the 5 per cent level of significance. When the test statistic is a continuous random variable as it is here, *the level of significance*, α, is the probability of rejecting H, given that H is actually true. Notice that this kind of chi-square test can be used for any number of categories with hypothetically given probabilities.

9.4 Cross-tabulation

Sometimes two or more variables are involved simultaneously in a classification. Suppose, for instance, that we want to study the possible relationship between the level of education of customers and the interest in a certain product. The data can be *cross-tabulated* as shown in Table 9.2. Here the level of education and the interest in the product have been classified into the two categories 'low' and 'high'. (More categories could have been used for each variable.) Notice that the figures in Table 9.2 are *very* special and have been chosen to demonstrate important features.

Table 9.2 Cross-tabulation of two variables

Interest in product	Level of education		Total
	Low	High	
High	53% (40)	48% (60)	50% (100)
Low	47% (35)	52% (65)	50% (100)
Total	100% (75)	100% (125)	100% (200)

Table 9.3 Cross-tabulation of three variables

Interest in product	Sex				Total
	Female		Male		
	Level of education		Level of education		
	Low	High	Low	High	
High	80% (20)	80% (20)	40% (20)	40% (40)	50% (100)
Low	20% (5)	20% (5)	60% (30)	60% (60)	50% (100)
Total	100% (25)	100% (25)	100% (50)	100% (100)	100% (200)

We want to explain the interest in the product. This variable is therefore the *dependent variable*. Level of education is regarded as an *independent variable*, since this variable is used to explain the interest in the product. In Table 9.2 there is only one independent variable.

For categorical variables, or continuous variables that have been put into categorical form, cross-tabulation is one commonly used method of analysis. In its simplest form, only two variables are involved, so the table becomes a simple two-way table like Table 9.2. Typically, the categories of the dependent variable are assigned to the rows of the cross-tabulation, while the categories of the independent variables are assigned to the columns. If the categories of the variables can be quantified, they are often arranged in decreasing order down the page and in increasing order from left to right (the same directions as in a common coordinate system with two axes).

In the cells of Table 9.2 the percentages which sum to 100 for each category of the independent variable give the most important information. Also the counts (frequencies) are shown in parentheses, since they will aid our discussion here. But the total count (total sample size) should *always* be recorded, since it is needed for judging reliability and performing statistical tests. The cross-tabulation can be interpreted by analyzing the pattern of percentages across each row. In the first row, we see that 53 per cent of the persons with low educational level show high interest in the product, while only 48 per cent of the persons with a high educational level show high interest. In the second row, the tendency is the opposite. Thus there is a (not necessarily statistically significant) relationship between level of education and interest in the product. It is very important, however, to notice that an observed association between variables may be *spurious*, i.e. not valid, even if it is statistically significant. This may especially occur if the dependent variable is not logically related to the independent one.

If a second independent variable is added to the analysis, a new table can be constructed and the situation may appear different. Suppose, for instance, that the variable 'sex' is included in Table 9.2. It is then conceivable (although unlikely) to obtain the figures shown in Table 9.3.

Notice that in Table 9.3 level of education seems to have no influence on the interest in the product. Sex now explains all the differences.

Conclusions based on a cross-tabulation may appear untenable when additional variables are introduced.

Our example is very special. In most cases, both independent variables will seem to have some effect on the dependent variable. In addition, there may be interaction between the independent variables. *Interaction* means that the effect of a level of one variable (the effect of a high level of education) depends on the particular level of the other variable (whether males or females are considered).

Further splittings of the tables are possible with more independent variables but, usually, at most three or four variables altogether are used. The main reason for this is that the cell counts of some cells will otherwise often be very small or zero because more and more unique cells are being created.

In tables like Table 9.2, with any number of row categories and any number of column categories, we are often interested in testing the hypothesis, H, that there is *statistical independence* between the row classification and the column classification. The alternative, A, is that there is dependence. An example of a computer print-out from such a test is shown below (expected counts are printed below observed counts):

	Low	High	Total
1	40	60	100
	37.50	62.50	
2	35	65	100
	37.50	62.50	
Total	75	125	200

$$\text{ChiSq} = 0.167 + 0.100 +$$
$$0.167 + 0.100 = 0.533$$

d.f. $= 1$

Using the level of significance 0.05, the critical value for 1 degree of freedom is 3.841. Since 0.533 is smaller than 3.841, H can not be rejected and *the conclusion is that there is independence.*

The above testing procedure is often called the *test of independence.* This term is appropriate when, in tables like Table 9.2, the researcher has determined the sample size in the lower-right corner of the table (200 in our example), while all other figures in the table have been determined by the sampling process (a cross-sectional study). In such cases, both 'interest in the product' and 'level of education' are *dependent variables.* A somewhat different situation emerges if the researcher determines deliberately how many persons with low education (75) and how many persons with high education (125) should be included in the sample.

Actually the whole bottom row of the table is then determined by the researcher, while all the other figures in the table are determined by the sampling process. It is then appropriate to regard 'level of education' as an *independent variable* and 'interest in the product' as the *dependent variable*. The appropriate hypothesis, H, now is that the conditional probabilities of high and low interest in the product, respectively, are the same, regardless of the level of education. The test of this hypothesis is often called *test of homogeneity*. The alternative hypothesis is that the conditional probabilities mentioned above are not the same. With regard to computation, degrees of freedom and critical values, the test of homogeneity and the test of independence are identical.

> The test of independence and the test of homogeneity are computationally completely equivalent. The goodness of fit test is different.

This chi-square test can also be used as an exploratory or descriptive device in connection with cross-tabulation of *several variables*, as in Table 9.3. A more satisfactory method is to use categorical data analysis (log-linear models).

To provide data to be used for illustrations in the following, we present a data matrix for a random sample of $n = 30$ individuals from a particular population in Table 9.4. The variables have been given names as well as symbols. The observations of each variable have been put into a column in the spreadsheet of the computer, such that variable x_1 is in the first column, variable x_2 is in the second, and so on. A brief explanation of symbols follows, where you will find (1) an x-symbol, (2) a name with at most eight characters, and (3) a brief explanation of the variable, if necessary:

x_1 = PersonNO = Person number
x_2 = Sex (1 if male, 2 if female)
x_3 = Age
x_4 = Degree (1 if no degree, 2 if undergraduate, 3 if graduate)
x_5 = IncomeLY = Income last year
x_6 = Income = Income present year
x_7 = ProductA = rating of product A on a scale from -3 to 3
x_8 = ProductB = rating of product B on a scale from -3 to 3
x_9 = BoughtPP (1 if bought product P when offered, 0 if not)

Notice that some missing values have been replaced by the missing value code, '$*$'.

Using a statistical computer package, various other useful tables can be derived from a table like Table 9.4. We will not pursue this here. But it is easy to get various frequency tables for a single variable, or a contingency table for two variables. Another possibility is to construct a table showing, for instance, mean income for all combinations of Degree and Sex.

Table 9.4 Data matrix

x_1	x_2	x_3	x_4	x_5	x_6	x_7	x_8	x_9
1	2	48	2	228	224	−1	3	0
2	2	62	1	213	225	3	1	0
3	1	36	2	257	271	−2	2	1
4	1	43	1	233	242	3	0	0
5	1	62	3	312	328	2	1	1
6	1	51	2	267	282	3	−2	1
7	1	37	3	194	228	3	1	0
8	1	45	2	283	284	1	1	1
9	1	*	2	188	214	2	2	0
10	2	30	2	269	276	3	−1	1
11	2	64	2	237	249	1	2	0
12	*	31	2	167	173	3	0	0
13	2	42	2	207	204	2	0	0
14	2	39	3	301	304	2	2	1
15	1	52	1	221	244	2	3	0
16	2	42	2	229	217	3	−1	0
17	2	56	2	181	182	2	−1	0
18	2	57	1	236	247	2	−1	0
19	2	47	1	233	244	−3	2	0
20	2	58	3	233	236	2	3	0
21	2	45	2	229	227	1	1	0
22	1	39	1	235	245	2	−3	0
23	2	47	2	274	272	3	2	1
24	1	46	1	199	196	2	1	0
25	2	32	1	130	122	−2	0	0
26	2	40	*	232	238	0	−1	*
27	2	31	1	159	162	3	−3	0
28	2	38	2	227	239	−2	1	0
29	1	50	3	399	410	3	−3	1
30	1	56	2	260	292	3	1	1

9.5 Two-sample problems regarding population means

Suppose that we want to find out whether income has increased from the last year to the present on the basis of variables x_5 (IncomeLY) and x_6 (Income) in Table 9.4. This is often called a two-sample problem with *paired observations*. They are paired because the observations of x_5 and x_6 occur in a pair for each individual. To solve this problem, we subtract the values of x_5 from the corresponding values of x_6 and place the difference in, say, column number 10. The differences can be regarded as values of a variable which we will denote by x_{10}. The differences are printed out below. The figures are to be read row by row from left to right, beginning with -4, 12, 14, etc. and ending with 11 and 32.

C10

-4	12	14	9	16	15	34	1	26	7
12	6	-3	3	23	-12	1	11	11	3
-2	10	-2	-3	-8	6	3	12	11	32

Notice that the differences, x_{10}, are comparable to the one-sample observations (number of cars per household) discussed earlier, so that the same methods apply.

The hypothesis, H, is that the population mean of differences, like the 30 differences in column 10, is equal to zero. The alternative, A, is that the population mean is greater than zero. Here, and later in this chapter, we assume that the level of significance $\alpha = 0.05$ has been chosen. The computer print-out from a Student's t-test is shown below:

TEST OF MU = 0.00 VERSUS MU GREATER THAN 0.00

	N	MEAN	STDEV	SE MEAN	T	P-VALUE
x_{10}	30	8.13	10.91	1.99	4.08	0.0002

The computed t-statistic is 4.08. The corresponding P-value, 0.0002, is smaller than 0.05, and therefore H is rejected. The conclusion is that the increase in income is significantly different from zero.

Methods based upon the Student's t-distribution require that some basic random variable(s), in this case a random difference, is approximately *normally distributed*. But the methods are quite robust, i.e. they usually work well, even if the normality assumption is not fulfilled. Several useful *non-parametric methods* are also available as alternatives to the classical t-methods. These have the advantage of requiring less in terms of assumptions. But if the assumptions necessary for using the t-methods are valid, the t-methods may be preferable, since they may be more powerful by, for instance, giving narrower confidence intervals than the corresponding non-parametric methods. Notice that methods based upon the t-distribution are concerned with means, while non-parametric methods are often concerned with medians. But if a distribution is symmetric, the mean and the median will coincide.

A simple non-parametric test applicable for the income problem is the *sign test*. Computer output from a sign test performed on the 30 values of x_{10} is shown below:

SIGN TEST OF MEDIAN = 0.00000 VERSUS G.T. 0.00000

	N	BELOW	EQUAL	ABOVE	P-VALUE	MEDIAN
x_{10}	30	7	0	23	0.0026	8.000

This test is based on the fact that 7 of the differences are negative and 23 are positive. No other information contained in the data is utilized. The *P*-value again indicates a significant difference between this year's income and last year's.

The sign test throws away some of the information contained in the data. A non-parametric test which also takes into account the relative sizes of the differences is the *Wilcoxon signed-rank test*. Computer output from this test for the income data is shown below:

TEST OF MEDIAN = 0.000000 VERSUS MEDIAN GREATER THAN 0.000000

	N	N FOR TEST	WILCOXON STATISTIC	P-VALUE	ESTIMATED MEDIAN
x_{10}	30	30	398.5	0.000	7.500

Once more, the *P*-value indicates a statistically significant increase in income since last year. This test is preferable to the sign test.

Next, we consider a problem with *unpaired observations*. Suppose we want to test the hypothesis, H, that, in the population, income is the same for men and women, against the alternative, A, that income is lower for women. Since we are not in a position to compare the income of a man with, say, the income of his wife, or his sister, we have unpaired observations. A conventional *t*-test is typically based on the assumption that the standard deviations are equal in the two populations from which the samples are drawn. Below we show computer output from a modified *t*-test and *t*-based confidence interval computation where this assumption is not necessary (Minitab Inc., 1993: 14−17):

TWOSAMPLE T FOR Income

Sex	N	MEAN	STDEV	SE MEAN
2	17	227.5	43.1	10
1	12	269.7	57.4	17

95 PCT CONFIDENCE INTERVAL FOR MU 2 − MU 1: $(-83, -1)$

TTEST MU 2 = MU 1 (VS LESS THAN): T = −2.15 P = 0.022 DF = 19

The *P*-value, 0.022, is smaller than 0.05, and thus H is rejected. The conclusion is that women earn less than men in this population.

A non-parametric alternative to this method is the *Mann−Whitney test* (Minitab Inc., 1993: 18−8). Print-out is shown below:

Mann−Whitney Confidence Interval and Test

Men	N = 12	Median =	258.00
Women	N = 17	Median =	236.00

Point estimate for ETA1−ETA2 is   33.50
95.1 Percent C.I. for ETA1−ETA2 is $(-0.99, 66.99)$

W = 223.5
Test of ETA1 = ETA2 vs. ETA1 > ETA2 is significant at 0.0285
The test is significant at 0.0284 (adjusted for ties)

The results are similar for the two methods, the *P*-values being 0.022 and 0.0285. Also, the confidence intervals are not very different if we make them comparable. To do so, we can, for instance, compare (1, 83) and (-0.99, 66.99), i.e. we must interchange signs and order of presentation for one of the intervals, since the differences happen to have been taken in different directions.

In problems involving one or two population means, *t*-methods are usually appropriate, but non-parametric methods are good alternatives.

Using *one-way analysis of variance*, we can test the hypothesis that all three categories of the variable x_4 (Degree) have the same mean income in the population. We assume that the variance of the income variable is the same for all categories. Here, x_6 = Income is the dependent variable and x_4 is the independent variable, if we use such terms. The resulting analysis of variance table is shown below:

ANALYSIS OF VARIANCE ON Income

SOURCE	DF	SS	MS	F	P
Degree	2	24547	12273	5.41	0.011.
ERROR	26	58963	2268		
TOTAL	28	83510			

The *P*-value 0.011 shows that the hypothesis must be rejected.
   A non-parametric alternative to this test is the *Kruskal—Wallis test*. Computer output is shown below:

29 CASES WERE USED
   1 CASE CONTAINED MISSING VALUES

LEVEL	NOBS	MEDIAN	AVE. RANK	Z VALUE
1	9	242.0	11.4	-1.51
2	15	239.0	14.9	-0.09
3	5	304.0	21.8	1.96
OVERALL	29		15.0	

H = 4.76 d.f. = 2 P = 0.093
H = 4.76 d.f. = 2 P = 0.093 (adjusted for ties)

The *P*-value of 0.093 shows that the hypothesis of equal medians *cannot* be rejected. Thus the two methods give essentially *different conclusions*.

This situation is not quite uncommon in statistics. In such situations, you ought to check whether the assumptions of each method seem to be fulfilled. The one-way analysis of variance is based upon assumptions of normal distributions and equal variances for income in each degree category. If these assumptions seem to be reasonably well fulfilled, the results might be trusted, since the method uses most of the information contained in the data. We could use normal score plots and tests of equality of variances found in the literature in order to test the assumptions, but the final conclusion may remain dubious.

9.6   Simple linear regression

One of the most useful statistical methods is *regression analysis*. We will present the essentials in a simplified example with only six observations and one-digit figures. Suppose a car dealer collects data for six months on four variables, $x_1 - x_3$ and y, and puts the values into columns $1-4$ of a computer data matrix in the same order. The variables are named and defined below:

x_{1j} = TV-Ads = Number of TV-ads applied by the car dealer in month number j.
x_{2j} = PaperAds = Number of paper-ads applied by the car dealer in month number j.
x_{3j} = Comp.Ads = Number of competitive ads in month number j.
y_j = CarSales = Number of cars sold (unit: 10) by the car dealer in month number j.

The car dealer expects CarSales to be positively correlated with TV-Ads and PaperAds. The correlation between CarSales and Comp.Ads is probably negative. But if the advertising of the competitors expands the whole market rather than just changing market shares, the correlation might be positive. The values of the four variables are shown below:

ROW	TV-Ads	PaperAds	Comp.Ads	CarSales
1	0	1	2	1
2	1	0	0	1
3	2	2	4	2
4	2	3	6	3
5	3	3	3	4
6	4	3	0	4

First, we explain the essentials of *simple linear regression* by assuming that only TV-Ads and CarSales have been observed. We now regard *CarSales* as the *dependent variable* and *TV-Ads* as the *independent variable*. A natural starting point is to plot CarSales against TV-Ads. A plot is shown in Figure 9.2.

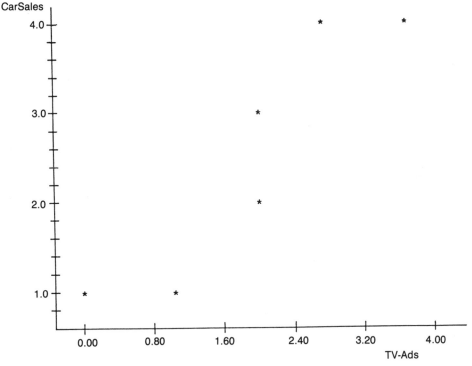

Figure 9.2 Scatter plot of CarSales against TV-Ads

The diagram shows a clear tendency of linear relationship between TV-Ads and CarSales. This is also verified by computing the correlation coefficient between the two variables, which is 0.923.

Next, we estimate the simple linear regression function of CarSales on TV-Ads. A computer print-out is shown below:

The regression equation is
CarSales = 0.700 + 0.900 TV-Ads

Predictor	COEF	STDEV	T-RATIO	P
Constant	0.7000	0.4453	1.57	0.191
TV-Ads	0.9000	0.1871	4.81	0.009

s = 0.5916   R-sq = 85.3%   R-sq(adj) = 81.6%

The estimated constant term 0.7000 shows that, if the dealer does not use TV-advertising at all (TV-Ads = 0), the estimated expected value of CarSales is 0.7 units, i.e. 7 cars. The estimated regression coefficient of CarSales on TV-Ads is 0.9000. This coefficient shows that, if the variable TV-Ads is increased by 1 unit, the estimated expected value of

CarSales increases by 0.9 units, i.e. 9 cars. This is useful information to the car dealer. But he should be reluctant to *extrapolate*, i.e. he should preferably not use this information for values of TV-Ads outside the interval from 0 to 4 which is covered by the sample.

The result, R-sq = 85.3 per cent, shows that the *sample determination coefficient* r^2 is equal to 0.853. Practically speaking, this means that the variation in the variable TV-Ads has *explained 85.3 per cent* of the variations in the variable CarSales in our sample. r^2 is the square of the sample correlation coefficient, r. The *P*-value, 0.009, of the estimated regression coefficient, b, of CarSales on TV-Ads is smaller than $\alpha = 0.05$, which we assume is our conventionally chosen level of significance. This means that we can reject the hypothesis, H, that the corresponding population regression coefficient, β, is equal to 0, using a two-sided alternative, A_2: $\beta \neq 0$. (A two-sided alternative is the default of the computer program used.)

The conclusion, then, is that TV-Ads and CarSales are significantly related to each other. Since it is close to impossible that increased advertising will result in decreased sales, it is indeed appropriate to use a one-sided alternative, A_1: $\beta > 0$ here.[2] This means that the *P*-value computed by the computer program should be divided by 2. Thus the relevant *P*-value is (0.009/2) = 0.0045. This represents even more evidence that there is a relationship between TV-Ads and CarSales.

In certain cases, as we shall see later, a coefficient may not turn out to be significantly different from zero when we use a two-sided alternative, although it proves to be significantly different from zero if a one-sided alternative is stated. Thus it is important to choose a one-sided alternative when appropriate.

A variable is useful if its *P*-value is smaller than α. Using a one-sided alternative instead of a two-sided means that the actual *P*-value will be halved.

Below, we have printed out several variables related to this problem:

ROW	CarSales	TV-Ads	StandRes	Fits	Residual
1	1	0	0.77033	0.7	0.3
2	1	1	−1.18431	1.6	−0.6
3	2	2	−0.92582	2.5	−0.5
4	3	2	0.92582	2.5	0.5
5	4	3	1.18431	3.4	0.6
6	4	4	−0.77033	4.3	−0.3

The *fits* are the *estimated expected car sales* or *predicted car sales* corresponding to the values of the independent variable TV-Ads found in the sample. The *residuals* are the corresponding deviations from the estimated regression line. Notice that the equation *Fit + Residual = CarSales* is valid for each month (each observation). We like the fits to be close to CarSales and the residuals to be close to 0. Then r^2 will be close to 1.

Regression analysis is based upon certain *assumptions*. It is sound practice to check these assumptions, but we do not think you should be too afraid of the assumptions not being fulfilled. Your results may be useful even if the standard assumptions are not all met, but then the results are typically more uncertain than the various statistics indicate. The most important thing is that you use sound judgement at all stages and that you know what you are doing.

Let us briefly show how some of the assumptions may be checked in our example. It should be remembered, however, that we have too few observations to get a realistic situation. The assumption of a *linear* model may be checked visually by looking at the plot in Figure 9.2. Several assumptions can be related to the unobservable *disturbances* which are 'estimated' by the *residuals*. The residuals can be plotted in several ways — for instance, against the independent variable. We may check visually the assumption of *homoscedasticity*, i.e. we check that the variance of the disturbance term does not change when the value of the independent variable changes. We would like to see a picture where the variation up and down in the diagram is roughly the same in, say, the left, the middle and the right part of the diagram.

To get some idea of the appropriateness of the assumption of *normally distributed disturbances*, you can, if you have more observations than we have, examine whether the resulting histogram of the residuals has some resemblance to the normal density. You can also use a normal probability plot (Minitab Inc., 1993: 13 − 18 and 13 − 19). If the points in the resulting diagram of *normal scores* fall roughly in a straight line, the residuals (and hopefully also the disturbances) seem to come from a normal population. The correlation coefficient tells how straight the line is.

If, as here, the data are time series data, there may be *autocorrelation* in the disturbances. In our example, the Durbin−Watson statistic is 1.89. If the D−W statistic is close to 2, as here, there is no danger of autocorrelation. If it is closer to 0, there may be positive autocorrelation. If it is closer to 4, there may be negative autocorrelation (more seldom). For critical values and further details, see, for instance, Gujarati (1988: chapter 12).

We probably also want to draw the estimated regression line together with our observations. This can be done, and the result for our example is shown in Figure 9.3.

We can now use a pen and draw the line through the points marked 'B'. Because of rounding errors in the diagram, the Bs may not lie exactly on a straight line. The '2' in the diagram indicates that two Bs coincide.

If we want to use simple linear regression, we may, in our example, regress y on x_1, as already done. But we may also regress y on x_2 or y on x_3. In choosing between various regression functions in situations like this, it is useful to look at the correlation coefficients. We may get the correlation coefficients either in a triangular table or in a true matrix (the brackets are lacking here). This is illustrated below:

	TV-Ads	PaperAds	Comp.Ads
PaperAds	0.783		
Comp.Ads	−0.060	0.472	
CarSales	0.923	0.918	0.155

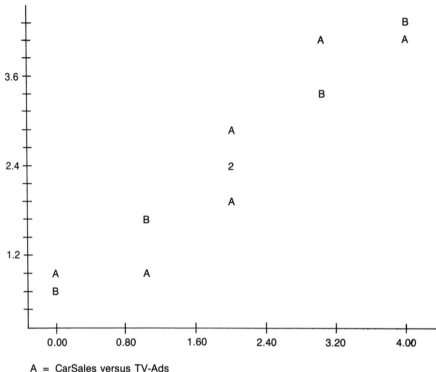

A = CarSales versus TV-Ads
B = Fits versus TV-Ads

Figure 9.3 Scatter plot and points on the regression line

1.00000	0.78262	−0.06030	0.92338
0.78262	1.00000	0.47194	0.91766
−0.06030	0.47194	1.00000	0.15467
0.92338	0.91766	0.15467	1.00000

We notice that among the three independent variables, TV-Ads is the one which has the highest sample correlation with the dependent variable CarSales. Previously, we found that the corresponding regression function seems to be satisfactory in all respects. Therefore, if we decide to use only one independent variable, TV-Ads is chosen.

9.7 Multiple regression

Multiple regression is an extremely powerful technique. A lot can be written about this tool, but, simply stated, it is by and large a straightforward generalization of simple regression. The most important difference is that we get more terms on the right-hand side of the equals sign in the regression function. Let us start estimating a regression function with three independent variables, as shown in the computer print-out below:

The regression equation is
CarSales = 0.491 + 0.333 TV-Ads + 0.795 PaperAds − 0.099 Comp.Ads

Predictor	COEF	STDEV	T-RATIO	P
Constant	0.4912	0.4073	1.21	0.351
TV-Ads	0.3333	0.3587	0.93	0.451
PaperAds	0.7953	0.4540	1.75	0.222
Comp.Ads	−0.0994	0.1527	−0.65	0.582

$s = 0.4393$ R-sq = 95.9%   R-sq(adj) = 89.8%

Analysis of Variance

SOURCE	DF	SS	MS	F	P
Regression	3	9.1140	3.0380	15.74	0.060
Error	2	0.3860	0.1930		
Total	5	9.5000			

We see that R-sq = 95.9 per cent, which indicates that almost 96 per cent of the variation in car sales in our sample has been explained by the three independent variables. This is good, but we would like to have an equation where the coefficients of all independent variables are *significantly different from zero*. This means that we would like the P-values of all the coefficients (except the constant term) to be smaller than our chosen level of significance, 0.05. Looking at the P-values next to the t-ratios, we see that none of them is smaller than $\alpha = 0.05$. Even if we use two-sided alternatives and divide the P-values by 2, we do not get significance. From a pure statistical point of view, we would therefore not accept using this equation.

The coefficients of the independent variables in an estimated multiple regression function are called estimated *partial regression coefficients*. They are usually denoted by $\hat{\beta}$ or b with appropriate subscripts. We will use b. The corresponding t-tests referred to above are called *partial t-tests* and are based upon the assumption that the coefficients of the other variables in the equation are different from zero in the population. As stated above, when a partial t-test shows significance (small P-value), we say that the corresponding coefficient is significantly different from zero. The F-statistic, $F_H = 15.74$, in the *analysis of variance table* can be used to test the hypothesis, H, that the coefficients of all the independent variables in the function are equal to zero in the population, against the alternative, A, that not all are equal to zero. Since the P-value is $0.06 > \alpha = 0.05$, we cannot reject H. Should we then drop the whole regression project? No, here it is appropriate to use *one-sided alternatives* for at least two of the coefficients. Allowing for this, the conclusion will be different, as will be shown later. The F-test assumes two-sided alternatives.

In a problem like the one here, with several potential independent variables, we have several regression functions to choose from. If the number of independent variables is k, the number of possible regression functions is $2^k - 1$. In our example, $k = 3$, and thus we have seven functions to choose from. As independent variables we can use x_1, or x_2, or x_3, or x_1 and x_2, or x_1 and x_3, or x_2 and x_3, or x_1, x_2 and x_3. The best we can do in a situation like this is usually to experiment with the various possibilities until we find the most satisfactory regression function. In doing this, we should try to get small P-values for the regression coefficients and a high R^2. In addition, you should check that the estimated regression coefficients have signs that do not contradict our prior knowledge. Thus, a positive regression coefficient of demand on price in a demand equation would seem strange in most situations.

Returning to our estimated multiple regression function above, we notice that the variable Comp.Ads has the highest P-value, namely 0.582. Let us drop this variable from the regression function. Then we would get the following results:

The regression equation is
CarSales = 0.371 + 0.516 TV-Ads + 0.548 PaperAds

Predictor	COEF	STDEV	T-RATIO	P
Constant	0.3710	0.3263	1.14	0.338
TV-Ads	0.5161	0.2006	2.57	0.082
PaperAds	0.5484	0.2243	2.45	0.092

s = 0.3949   R-sq = 95.1%   R-sq(adj) = 91.8%

Analysis of Variance

SOURCE	DF	SS	MS	F	P
Regression	2	9.0323	4.5161	28.97	0.011
Error	3	0.4677	0.1559		
Total	5	9.5000			

We see that R^2 is almost as high as it was for the preceding function. This also indicates that Comp.Ads is not a very useful variable when the variables TV-Ads and PaperAds are also in the function. Looking at the P-values of the latter two variables, we find that they are still greater than our chosen level of significance, $\alpha = 0.05$. However, assuming that neither TV advertising nor paper advertising has a negative influence on sales, the appropriate alternatives in testing that the population coefficients are equal to zero are *one-sided*. Thus, the recorded P-values are not the relevant ones. The correct P-values are $0.082/2 = 0.041$ for TV-Ads and $0.092/2 = 0.046$ for PaperAds. Since both P-values are smaller than 0.05, the conclusion is that both coefficients are significantly different from zero. We notice that both coefficients have positive signs, which seems reasonable. We also notice that $R^2 = 0.951$, which is a high figure. The conclusion, therefore, is that this seems to be a good function to use.

Look for a function where all bs are significantly different from zero and have correct signs, and where R^2 is as high as possible.

If we want to check assumptions, we can do it in much the same way as for simple regression. The fits and residuals, together with the original variables, are shown below:

ROW	CarSales	TV-Ads	PaperAds	Fits	Residual
1	1	0	1	0.91935	0.080645
2	1	1	0	0.88710	0.112903
3	2	2	2	2.50000	−0.500000
4	3	2	3	3.04839	−0.048387
5	4	3	3	3.56452	0.435484
6	4	4	3	4.08065	−0.080645

Again, Fit + Residual = CarSales for any month.

Let us finally consider the following three determination coefficients:

$r_{y1}^2 = 0.92338^2 = 0.853$ (between CarSales and TV-Ads)
$r_{y2}^2 = 0.91766^2 = 0.842$ (between CarSales and PaperAds)
$R_{y.12}^2 = 0.951$ (between CarSales and the two independent variables TV-Ads and PaperAds)

The first coefficient indicates that, in our sample, the variations in TV advertising from month to month have explained 85.3 per cent of the variations in car sales from month to month. Similarly, the second coefficient expresses that the variations in paper advertising have explained 84.2 per cent of the variations in car sales. Adding these two percentages, we get 169.5 per cent. To say that the two independent variables together explain 169.5 per cent of the variations in car sales is, of course, nonsense. The reason why we get such a high figure is that the two independent variables are correlated with each other. As we have seen before, the sample correlation coefficient between them is $r_{12} = 0.78262$, which is a high figure.

A high figure is quite natural. In months when car dealers expect people to be very much interested in buying cars, they will, of course, advertise a lot, both on TV and in the newspapers. Conversely, in months when people usually buy few cars, car dealers will advertise little on TV and in the papers. Since the variables TV-Ads and PaperAds change together from month to month, they are competitors with regard to explaining the variation in car sales. Each of them can explain pretty much alone, but together they explain less than the sum of the respective percentages when they are alone. Actually, we see from the multiple determination coefficient, $R_{y.12}^2 = 0.951$, that the two independent variables together explain 95.2 per cent of the variation in car sales.

In general, when the independent variables are uncorrelated with each other in the sample, we say that they are *orthogonal*. This is desirable, because the regression analysis is greatly simplified, but this situation is quite unusual in business studies. If independent variables are perfectly correlated with each other in the sample, we say that we have *perfect multicolinearity*. This is a problem which must be resolved. In most cases, there is some correlation between the independent variables. Then we have some degree of multicolinearity, like we have in our example above. This makes regression analysis more difficult to perform and it causes our results to be less reliable, but we can still get very useful information from a regression analysis.

9.8   Dummy variables in regression analysis

9.8.1   Independent dummy variables

Dummy variables are a very useful device for making regression analysis even more powerful. A *dummy variable* is an artificial variable which can have only two or three values, usually the two values 0 and 1. By using dummy variables, two or more different sets of data can be analyzed as a single data set. The results for the various data sets can then be compared in a stringent way and statistical inference becomes more efficient.

As an example, suppose we consider two groups of sales persons. Group A has completed a thorough training programme, while group B has only been given a brief introduction to sales work. We want to perform a regression analysis. The independent variable is the number of months the person has been a sales person, and the dependent variable is monthly sales. Of course, it is possible to analyze group A and group B separately. By analyzing both groups together, using dummy variables, we can compare the performances of the two groups. Thus we can estimate possible differences between the groups and test whether the differences are significantly different from zero.

The data for our example are shown in Table 9.5. We have 10 observations for group B, shown in the upper part of the table. The 12 observations for group A have been placed below the data for group B. We use four variables:

x_{1j} = MonthAll = Number of months' experience as a sales person for person number j.

x_{2j} = Dummy = A variable with value 0 for all persons in group B, and 1 for all persons in group A.

x_{3j} = Interact = the product of x_{1j} and x_{2j}.

y_j = SalesAll = Sales per month last month by person number j.

We have used the ending 'All' in two names as a reminder that all observations for both groups are included.

In Figure 9.4, data for both groups have been plotted in the same diagram. There seems to be scatter around two lines, the line for group A being at a higher level than that for group B. Now, we estimate a multiple regression function of y on x_1 and x_2. The result is shown below:

The regression equation is

Table 9.5 Data including dummy variables

ROW	MonthAll	Dummy	Interact	SalesAll
1	2	0	0	3
2	5	0	0	1
3	7	0	0	4
4	10	0	0	2
5	13	0	0	4
6	15	0	0	6
7	20	0	0	5
8	23	0	0	9
9	25	0	0	7
10	29	0	0	8
11	4	1	4	8
12	6	1	6	11
13	7	1	7	15
14	13	1	13	14
15	15	1	15	20
16	21	1	21	18
17	22	1	22	22
18	25	1	25	28
19	30	1	30	26
20	33	1	33	33
21	32	1	32	26
22	28	1	28	22

SalesAll $= -2.52 + 0.498$ MonthAll $+ 13.0$ Dummy

Predictor	COEF	STDEV	T-RATIO	P
Constant	-2.520	1.424	-1.77	0.093
MonthAll	0.49801	0.06977	7.14	0.000
Dummy	12.976	1.360	9.54	0.000

$s = 3.079$ R-sq $= 90.8\%$ R-sq(adj) $= 89.8\%$

Both regression coefficients are significantly different from zero and the estimated multiple regression function has a very interesting interpretation.

Let us first consider persons belonging to group B. For such persons the dummy variable is always equal to zero and the last term disappears. We are then left with the simple regression function, SalesAll $= -2.52 + 0.498$ MonthAll for group B. Next, suppose that we consider persons belonging to group A. Then the dummy variable is always equal to 1 and the last term simply becomes 13.0 for all units. This term can, of course, be added to the constant term -2.52. Thus we get the simple regression function SalesAll $= 10.48 + 0.498$ MonthAll for group A.

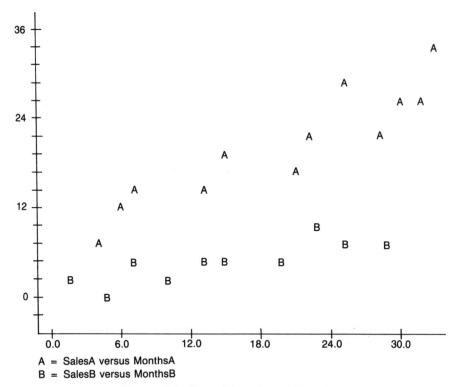

A = SalesA versus MonthsA
B = SalesB versus MonthsB

Figure 9.4 Plot of data from Table 9.5

We see that the coefficient of the dummy variable estimates the difference in sales level between the two groups. The estimated difference is 12.976. The P-value shows that the difference is significantly different from zero.

Taking a closer look at Figure 9.4, we notice that there seems to be a difference not only in *level*, but also in *slope*. The imagined line for group A seems to be steeper than the line for group B. Thus the model we have been using up to now is probably not quite appropriate. Below we have estimated a multiple regression function of y on x_1, x_2 and x_3:

The regression equation is
SalesAll = 1.21 + 0.248 MonthAll + 6.18 Dummy + 0.406 Interact

Predictor	COEF	STDEV	T-RATIO	P
Constant	1.211	1.516	0.80	0.435
MonthAll	0.24756	0.08801	2.81	0.012
Dummy	6.180	2.155	2.87	0.010
Interact	0.4062	0.1121	3.62	0.002

s = 2.405   R-sq = 94.7%   R-sq(adj) = 93.8%

Again, all regression coefficients are significantly different from zero, and R^2 is quite high.

Let us first consider persons belonging to group B. From Table 9.5 we see that both the variable Dummy and the variable Interact are equal to zero for these persons. Thus, we are left with the simple regression function SalesAll = 1.21 + 0.248 MonthAll for group B. The coefficient of the variable Dummy estimates the difference in level for the two groups in the same manner as before. Notice that, for group A, the variable Interact is identical to the variable MonthAll. This is seen from Table 9.5. Accordingly, the estimated regression function can be written as follows for group A: SalesAll = 1.21 + 0.248 MonthAll + 6.18 Dummy + 0.406 Interact = 1.21 + 0.248 MonthAll + 6.18(1) + 0.406 MonthAll = 7.39 + (0.248 + 0.406) MonthAll = 7.39 + 0.654 MonthAll. Again, we have a simple linear regression function.

The conclusion is that group A has a steeper regression line than group B. The difference in slope is estimated to be 0.406 and the corresponding P-value shows that the difference in slope is significantly different from zero. The difference in level will therefore vary with the value of the variable MonthAll, but when this variable has the value zero, the difference in level is estimated to be 6.18. Also this difference is significantly different from zero.

In general, if we have two groups, we need $(2 - 1) = 1$ dummy variable to compare the groups. If we have four groups (for instance, seasonal data for four quarters), we need $(4 - 1) = 3$ dummy variables to account for the differences between the seasons. The dummy variable D_2 may have the value 1 for the second quarter and 0 for all other quarters. The variable D_3 may have the value 1 for the third quarter and 0 for the other quarters, while the variable D_4 may have the value 1 for the fourth quarter and 0 for the other quarters. Other choices are also possible. Dummy variables are a very flexible tool. Actually, all kinds of analysis of variance can be stated in such a way that it becomes a regression analysis using only dummy variables.

Dummy variables permit subsets of the data to have regression functions with different intercepts and different slopes.

9.8.2 Dependent dummy variable

So far, our dummy variables have been *independent* variables. To let the *dependent* variable be a dummy variable is a very fascinating trick. The corresponding fits and predictions can then be interpreted as *probabilities*. For example, in Table 9.4, let x_9 = BoughtPP be the dependent variable. This variable has the value 0 for persons who did not buy product P, and 1 for those who bought that product. The independent variable could be x_6 = Income. The corresponding regression function is shown below:

The regression equation is

BoughtPP $= -1.24 + 0.00640$ Income

Predictor	COEF	STDEV	T-RATIO	P
Constant	-1.2431	0.2763	-4.50	0.000
Income	0.006400	0.001112	5.76	0.000

$s = 0.3212$ R-sq $= 55.1\%$ R-sq(adj) $= 53.5\%$

By plugging the income of a person into the estimated regression function above, we compute the estimated probability that the person will buy product P. The situation is similar if we have several independent variables. The use of a dummy dependent variable is useful when we want to find out why some people are unemployed and some are not, why some women work outside their homes while others do not, etc.

The use of a dummy variable as the dependent variable raises some problems, however:

- It can easily be shown that the disturbance term can have only two possible values for each value of the independent variable. Thus, the standard assumption of normally distributed disturbance terms is clearly not satisfied (non-normality).
- The standard assumption of equal variances for all disturbance terms is also clearly broken (heteroscedasticity). It can be shown that the variance of the disturbance term depends on the value of the independent variable.
- The probabilities estimated from a function like the one above may turn out to be *negative* or *larger than 1*. Thus, in our example, we get negative estimated probabilities for units number 12, 17, 25 and 27, while the estimated probability for unit number 29 is larger than 1. This is an indication that our linear model is not good.

We may simply choose to overlook these problems and still get useful results. However, non-normality and heteroscedasticity make the results more uncertain than the various statistical measures indicate. The natural thing to do with the negative estimates is to set them equal to 0, while the estimates which are greater than 1 are set equal to 1.

The use of *weighted least squares* is a means of dealing with the problem of heteroscedasticity. *Logistic regression*, which involves the logit transformation, represents an improved model and assures that the estimated probabilities do not fall outside the interval from 0 to 1. This, in connection with weighted least squares, is often a satisfactory procedure.

> Using a dummy dependent variable, you can predict the probability of membership in one of two groups as a function of independent variables.

9.9 Linear discriminant analysis

Discriminant analysis, like dependent dummy variable regression, deals with groups of units. Returning once more to Table 9.4, suppose we want to find out whether $x_3 = $ Age and x_6 = Income can be used to predict group membership, i.e. whether a person will buy product P or not. Here x_9 = BoughtPP is the dependent variable, while x_3 and x_6 are independent variables. Computer output from a discriminant analysis is shown below:

Linear Discriminant Analysis for BoughtPP

Group	0	1
Count	19	9

28 cases used   2 cases contain missing values

Summary of Classification

Put into	... True	Group ...
Group	0	1
0	19	0
1	0	9
Total N	19	9
N Correct	19	9
Proport.	1.000	1.000

N = 28   N Correct = 28   Prop. Correct = 1.000

Squared Distance Between Groups

	0	1
0	0.00000	7.42431
1	7.42431	0.00000

Linear Discriminant Function for Group

	0	1
Constant	-18.127	-31.758
Age	0.225	0.052
Income	0.120	0.203

Our data are very special and our aim here is just to illustrate the method. The output is mostly self-explanatory. From the 'Summary of Classification' we see that the analysis has put all units into the groups where they truly belong. This is usually not the case. The following two *linear discriminant functions* have been computed. For group 0: $F_0 = -18.127 + 0.225$ Age $+ 0.120$ Income. For group 1: $F_1 = -31.758 + 0.052$ Age $+ 0.203$ Income. These two can be used to predict whether a person, say of age 54 and with income 250, will buy product P. We simply plug these figures into the two functions and get $f_0(54,250) = 24.023$ and $f_1(54,250) = 21.800$. Since $f_0(54,250) > f_1(54,250)$, we predict that the person belongs to group 0, i.e. s/he will not buy the product.

By using subcommands we get additional output, some of which is shown below:

Summary of Classified Observations

Observation	True Group	Pred Group	Group	Sqrd Distnc	Probability
1	0	0	0	0.06104	0.969
			1	6.94746	0.031
2	0	0	0	3.028	0.997
			1	14.613	0.003
3	1	1	0	5.9264	0.074

Let us consider observation number 1. This observation truly belongs to group number 0 and has also correctly been classified into group number 0. The squared distance from this observation to the group centroid (mean point) of group 0 in the plane where x_1 and x_2 are coordinates is 0.06104, which is a small figure. The estimated probability of this observation belonging to group 0 is therefore a large figure, namely 0.969. On the other hand, the squared distance from this observation to the group centroid of group 1 is 6.94746, which is a large figure. The estimated probability of this observation belonging to group 1 is therefore a small figure, namely 0.031. The estimated probabilities are based upon the assumption that the independent variables follow a multivariate normal distribution. If a unit is classified into a group other than the one where it truly belongs, the unit is said to be *misclassified* and is marked in the computer output.

In Minitab, linear discriminant analysis works much the same way as shown above, even if we have more than two groups and/or more than two independent variables. If we have several groups, we may let the dependent variable have the value 1 for units belonging to group 1, the value 2 for units belonging to group 2, and so on. We get as many linear discriminant functions as we have groups. Plugging the values of the independent variables for a person into the various discriminant functions in turn, we find which function gives the highest value and thus into which group the analysis puts the person.

If we have several potential independent variables and wonder which of them to retain in a discriminant analysis, regression analysis may give us some guidelines. Notice also that we should be careful not to be too impressed by a high proportion of correctly classified units, i.e. by a high *hit ratio*. Suppose we have two groups, one consisting of 20 units and the other consisting of 80 units. If we arbitrarily classify all units into the larger group, we automatically get a hit ratio of 80 per cent! In any case, the hit ratio recorded in analyses like the one above is usually too optimistic because we classify the very data that we have used to compute the discriminant functions. A sound recommendation, which ought to be followed if we have a sufficiently large sample, is to divide the sample randomly into two groups, often called the analysis sample and the holdout sample. The *analysis sample* is used to compute the discriminant functions, while the *holdout sample* is used to test the validity of the functions.

Logistic regression is preferable to discriminant analysis when the independent variables are not multivariate normal.

9.10   Principal components analysis

Suppose that we have more variables than we can handle in an efficient way. If most of the variables are correlated with each other in the sample, *principal components analysis*, also called *PC analysis*, may be used as a data reduction technique. In order to understand this, we should remember that what is important with variables is the variation. Roughly speaking, if we take care of the variation from unit to unit in our variables, it does not matter much if we change units or combine variables. As an example, let us consider accounting data for the 70 largest savings banks in Norway at 31 December 1990. The variables are as follows:

x_1 = Capital = Total capital
x_2 = Loans = Gross loans
x_3 = Solidity = Equity
x_4 = Profits = Profits in 1990
x_5 = Losses = Losses on loans
x_6 = Reserves = Ordinary net reserves

These six variables will be called the *observed variables* or the original variables. Data for the six largest banks are printed below. The remaining observations are not printed, to save space.

ROW	Capital	Loans	Solidity	Profits	Losses	Reserves
1	82012.0	63057.0	5082.0	858.2	1476.0	−631.6
2	18139.0	13957.0	950.0	81.0	387.0	−304.0
3	17670.0	14695.0	1152.0	131.8	305.6	−173.8
4	16240.7	11605.0	1063.5	195.8	257.6	−62.5
5	11838.1	10297.9	629.2	281.9	453.9	−171.4
6	9192.7	7507.6	705.7	202.2	184.8	16.6

It is likely that these six variables give a pretty good picture of the economic situation of the banks and of the variation from bank to bank. One may ask, however, whether as many as six variables are necessary to describe this. Several of the variables are highly correlated as shown in the computer print-out of correlations below:

	Capital	Loans	Solidity	Profits	Losses
Loans	1.000				
Solidity	0.994	0.992			
Profits	0.964	0.966	0.961		
Losses	0.956	0.960	0.923	0.945	
Reserves	−0.841	−0.845	−0.780	−0.783	−0.940

Since the correlations are high, the situation is well fit for a PC analysis.

The principles of such an analysis can be explained as follows. Each of the six variables above has a sample variance. The sum of these sample variances is called the *total variance*. If we standardize the variables before the analysis starts, which is typically done, each variable gets a variance of 1, and thus the total variance is equal to 6 here. In the PC analysis, we create six new variables called *principal components*, or PCs. These are denoted PC1, PC2, . . ., PC6. Alternatively, we use the notation $Z_1, Z_2, . . ., Z_6$. The principal components satisfy the following conditions:

- Each PC is a linear combination (linear function without a constant term) of all the original variables. The coefficient of, for example, x_1 in the function defining PC1 is often called the *loading of PC1 on x_1*.
- All the PCs are uncorrelated with each other in the sample (i.e. orthogonal).
- Each PC has a sample mean equal to 0.
- The sample variance of PC1 is greater than or equal to the sample variance of PC2. The variance of PC2 is greater than or equal to the variance of PC3, and so on.
- The sum of the variances of the six PCs is equal to the *total variance* (total variance is preserved).
- For each PC, the sum of the squares of the loadings on the various observed variables is equal to 1. (This is true in standard PC analysis as in Minitab, but not necessarily always.)

Results of a PC analysis of our data are shown below:

Eigenanalysis of the Correlation Matrix

Eigenvalue	5.6237	0.3129	0.0601	0.0019	0.0010	0.0004
Proportion	0.937	0.052	0.010	0.000	0.000	0.000
Cumulative	0.937	0.989	0.999	1.000	1.000	1.000

Variable	PC1	PC2	PC3	PC4	PC5	PC6
Capital	−0.418	−0.177	−0.307	0.087	−0.382	0.739
Loans	−0.419	−0.164	−0.267	0.072	−0.525	−0.667
Solidity	−0.411	−0.362	−0.383	−0.139	0.726	−0.086
Profits	−0.409	−0.296	0.742	0.432	0.095	0.004
Losses	−0.415	0.260	0.347	−0.796	−0.071	0.029
Reserves	0.376	−0.810	0.133	−0.385	−0.192	0.020

We first consider the three rows denoted 'Eigenvalue', 'Proportion' and 'Cumulative'. Each of these three rows pertains to the six principal components listed below the rows, PC1, PC2, etc. *Eigenvalue* simply means sample variance in this context. Accordingly, the variance of PC1 is 5.6237. The variance of PC2 is smaller, namely 0.3129, and so on. The sum of the six eigenvalues is 6, the total variance. *Proportion* means proportion of total variance. Thus, the variance of PC1 is 93.7 per cent of total variance. The

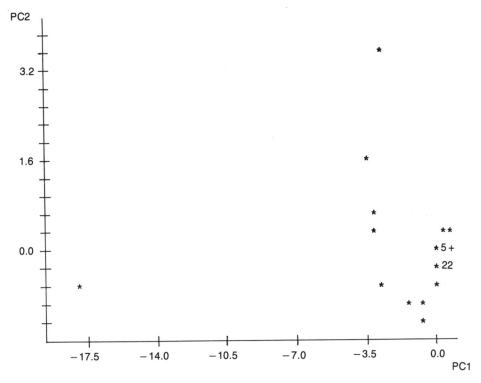

Figure 9.5 Plot of PC2 against PC1

corresponding proportion for PC2 is much smaller, namely 5.2 per cent. *Cumulative* means cumulative proportion. Thus $0.937 + 0.052 = 0.989$. Further, $0.989 + 0.010 = 0.999$, and so on.

The print-out shows that the first principal component, PC1, accounts for 93.7 per cent of the total variance. If we are willing to sacrifice 6.3 per cent of the information in the original variables, we can drop all the principal coefficients but the first one. *PC1 alone can then be used to describe the variation between the banks.* We can then regard PC1 as a kind of index or average of all the original variables. This is what we mean by *data reduction.*

If we would like to take care of more of the information in the original variables, we can use the first two principal components. These account for 98.9 per cent of the total variance, practically all of the variation. It is thus quite clear that, instead of using six observed variables, it is sufficient to use the first two principal components. The banks can be described quite satisfactorily in terms of these variables. We can, for instance, plot PC2 against PC1 as shown in Figure 9.5.

Figure 9.5 shows that most of the banks are found in the lower-right corner of the diagram. But we find one bank in the lower-left corner and some banks in the upper-right corner. Examining these banks further, we may find interesting features. Often, in such cases, we can use a methodology called *cluster analysis* to group the banks into clusters.

Notice that the eigenanalysis is based upon the *correlation matrix* of the original variables. This is the default in some computer packages and is equivalent to using standardized variables. To standardize a variable means to subtract the mean from each value and then divide each difference by the standard deviation of the variable. It is also possible to let the eigenanalysis be based upon the covariance matrix of the original variables. This is equivalent to only centring (and not standardizing) the original variables. To centre a variable means to subtract its mean from all its values.

As a matter of fact, PC analysis is arbitrary in the sense that the result will depend on whether we use the correlation matrix or the covariance matrix. If we use the covariance matrix, the result will also depend on the units in which the original variables are measured. Unless we have variables which are measured in the same units and are roughly of the same kind and magnitude, the safest procedure is probably to use the correlation matrix.

Mathematically, principal components can be interpreted as new axes or dimensions in a space with as many dimensions as there are original variables. The principal components are found by rotating the coordinate system, keeping the axes at right angles to each other. The loadings of each principal component on the various original variables are shown in the print-out above. If a principal component has high loadings on a group of related variables and low loadings on the other original variables, we may give that principal component a name and interpretation corresponding to the group with high loadings. Very often we are not able to do so, and this abstract nature of the principal components is one of the drawbacks of PC analysis.

> One common rule says that principal components with eigenvalues > 1 should be retained.

9.11   Factor analysis

Factor analysis has much in common with principal components analysis. The main purpose is again data reduction and interpretation. Principal components analysis can be considered a special case of factor analysis. The observed variables in a factor analysis must be *ratio- or interval-scaled*. One important difference between PC analysis and factor analysis is that the principal components are linear functions of the original variables. In factor analysis, on the other hand, the intention is to express the original variables as linear functions of unknown factors. These unknown factors or variables are of two kinds, namely common factors and unique or specific factors. A *common factor* can be thought of as an unknown variable that influences at least two of the original variables. It can be compared to an independent variable in multiple regression analysis.

A *unique factor* or *specific factor* can be compared to the disturbance term in a multiple regression function. It influences only one of the original variables.

The model of a common factor analysis consists of as many equations as there are original variables. Each equation can be compared to a multiple regression equation. Formally, all common factors are usually included on the right-hand side of each equation. Some of the factors, however, can have coefficients that are equal to zero in some equations, but each common factor must have coefficients that are different from zero in at least two equations. If this is not the case, the common factor in reality turns out to become a part of a unique factor.

The coefficients of the various factors in the equation of a particular original variable are called the *loadings* of that original variable on the various factors. The loadings are actually identical with the corresponding correlation coefficients between the various factors and the original variable. The number of common factors is smaller than or at most equal to the number of original variables. If the number of common factors is equal to the number of original variables, all unique factors will be equal to zero and the system of equations in the factor model has a unique solution. If, in a situation of this kind, we solve the system of equations with regard to the common factors, we end up with a principal component analysis. In this case, the common factors correspond to the principal components. For further details on factor analysis, see Hair (1992).

> Factor solutions are often rotated to get loadings close to one or zero. This makes interpretation easier.

9.12 Other methods of analysis

So far in this chapter we have shown examples of ways of analyzing data. Many more methods of analysis are available, however. A brief overview of some other multivariate techniques is given below. There is a vast literature on data analysis in general and multivariate analysis in particular. A good introduction to multivariate data analysis for readers with a limited background in mathematics and statistics is found in Hair (1992). Another useful text, using more mathematics, is the well-known textbook by Johnson and Wichern (1992). In these books you will find further useful references.

The objective of *cluster analysis* is to discover natural groupings of the units in a sample. Each resulting group is called a *cluster*. The beginner may easily confuse cluster analysis with discriminant analysis. One very important difference is that in discriminant analysis the groups and the group memberships of the various units are known before the analysis starts. In cluster analysis, on the contrary, we do not have any groups at all at the outset. On the basis of the data for the *n* units in the sample, groups are created.

In business studies, grouping or clustering of units is often useful and can help in generating hypotheses to be tested later. One example is to cluster customers into clusters which are market segments consisting of similar customers. Another application is to group brands of a product into clusters consisting of similar brands. The grouping is based upon similarities or distances (dissimilarities) in an n-dimensional space.

The basic idea of *multidimensional scaling* or MDS can be illustrated as follows. Suppose we are given a table listing the distances between all pairs of capitals for all the countries in Europe. This table could, for instance, be arranged as a symmetric matrix with zeros along the main diagonal. Only the upper or lower triangle of the matrix is needed. Using only this information, we are asked to construct a map of Europe showing the locations of all the capitals.

In principle, customers can express their attitudes regarding the distances between various brands by telling which pairs of brands are very similar and which pairs of brands are not so similar. This way we obtain data comparable to the distances between cities. The basic objective of MDS in this example is to map the brands in a multidimensional space in such a way that the relative positions of the brands reflect the perceived distances between the brands. Hopefully this can be done in few dimensions, because this will simplify interpretation.

Canonical correlation analysis is a technique for identifying and quantifying the associations between a set of x-variables on the one hand and a set of y-variables on the other. Multiple and simple correlation analysis can be considered as special cases of canonical correlation analysis where one or both sets contain a single variable. If we consider a variable related to a commodity like a car and a variable related to the person buying the car, we will, except for price and income, often find only a small correlation coefficient. Still, we have a definite feeling that persons with specific characteristics buy special kinds of car. In such situations, canonical correlation analysis may be useful.

Multivariate analysis of variance, often referred to as *MANOVA*, is a generalization of the usual univariate analysis of variance, ANOVA. The new aspect of MANOVA, compared to ANOVA, is that instead of comparing k group means for only one dependent variable, k group means for p dependent variables can be compared simultaneously.

As an example, suppose we want to compare prices for p different products in k different cities on a certain day, based upon random samples of n price observations for each product in each city. For each product we could, for instance, take a random sample of n stores from each city. Our data matrix would then consist of pkn observations altogether. Using ANOVA to test the hypothesis of equal population means in the k cities, we would have to perform p different analyses: one for each product. With MANOVA, a single analysis would be sufficient. Using the concept of a vector, MANOVA can be used to test the hypothesis that the k p-dimensional vectors of population means for the prices are the same for all k cities. Such a vector of population means is called a *centroid*. While with ANOVA we are testing that k population means are equal, with MANOVA the more general hypothesis being tested is that k population centroids are equal. Conceptually, the two procedures are similar.

To perform one MANOVA is in most cases a more powerful procedure than conducting p univariate ANOVAs. Group differences that are not revealed using several ANOVAs may be found using MANOVA. The reason is that MANOVA takes into account the correlations between the dependent variables (the prices in our example).

Interpretation of results may also be more meaningful using MANOVA. If the dependent variables are uncorrelated, however, there is nothing to gain by using MANOVA.

Notes

1. The term *column* here coincides with the term column in, for example, SAS or Minitab. However, an old-fashioned data card with 80 columns would not necessarily give room for as much as 80 of our columns.
2. We assume that the car dealer uses money in a rational way. He will not spend so much money advertising that potential customers get tired of seeing the firm's cars on TV. If he spends that much money, people may simply decide not to buy his cars.

CHAPTER 10

Writing the final report

After completing the data collection and data analysis, we have to put the research problem, the data collected and the findings into a logical, consistent and persuasive report. Fortunately, like research proposals and methodology, research reports conform to a fairly standard format.

Before starting to write the final report, we should consider the purpose of the report and to whom it is addressed. Research reports typically start with an executive summary providing the important parts of the report. After the summary, a *preface* is normally written where we explain the course of study and thank individuals and organizations who have been helpful in data collection, funding, etc.

The process of writing up a report is complex and tedious work. The report should be concise, and the findings and arguments presented in a convincing and consistent way. It is also important to present the research methodology and results in a such a way that the reader can judge the validity and relevance of the findings.

We should give an account of our methods' *weaknesses and strengths* and the necessary details so that readers can make their own judgements on the validity and reliability of our study and findings. We should convince the reader that we have, first of all, done our job as a researcher, investigating a certain problem area with systematic data collection and data analysis, presented in a logical, easy-to-read and understandable report. Second, we must show that we have followed the technically correct and consistent method expected of a qualified report, that our hypotheses and/or conclusions are properly supported by existing literature and empirical evidence, and that there is a logical congruence between different parts of the report. We should also be concerned that our report gives due credit to earlier studies we have used, and that we refer to all the sources in a proper manner. These two aspects are very important in qualified report writing and are therefore treated separately in this chapter.

10.1   Structure of the report

The following outline is a commonly used format for a research report. The chosen

	Page no.
SUMMARY	i
PREFACE	ii
1 INTRODUCTION	1
1.1 Purpose of the Study	3
1.2 Research Problem	3
. . .	

Figure 10.1 Example of a table of contents

format is, however, dependent upon the reader for whom the report is prepared. Our common format is as follows:

1. Title page.
2. Table of contents.
3. Executive summary.
4. Introduction and problem statement.
5. Theoretical background.
6. Methodology.
7. Findings or empirical study.
8. Conclusions and recommendations.
9. Footnotes.
10. Bibliography or references.
11. Appendix.

10.1.1 Title page

The title page should indicate the topic of research and the name(s) of the researcher(s) (authors). Second, it should indicate the name of the organization where the report has been prepared and for what programme if appropriate: for example, 'MBA Thesis for the Norwegian School of Management'. If it is a research project ordered or demanded by a company or any other organization, the company or organization's name should also appear on the title page. Moreover, if the project has received any financial help from an institute other than the school or university, this name should also appear on the title page.

10.1.2 Table of contents

The table of contents lists the contents of the report with page numbers. Here, the headings and subheadings are presented. The reader should be able to differentiate the headings and subheadings both in the table of contents and in the report (see Figure 10.1). The table of contents should also include tables and figures with pages numbered consecutively.

10.1.3   Executive summary

A summary provides the important aspects of each part of the report. It is often stated that a summary should be *self-sufficient* because most of the readers, especially business executives, often read only the summary (Churchill, 1991). The summary thus should highlight the whole report. However, it should be based on the main report and should not include any new material. The data we have collected, presented and analyzed in our report are often buried in the middle or at the end of our report and have to be brought forward in the summary so that the reader can quickly and without any trouble perceive the message of our report (Bolsky, 1988).

The length of a summary depends upon the complexity of the original material. Normally we should reduce the material in a summary to, at the most, 5 per cent of the report's full length, or a couple of pages.

10.1.4   Introduction and problem statement

An introduction to a research report should present what the study is about and what the purpose of the study is. This background will provide the reader with the necessary information to understand and comprehend the rest of the report. The objectives and the purpose of the study should be clearly mentioned in this section. After reading this section, the reader should have complete information on what the report deals with, why we are studying a particular problem and what can be expected to be found in the rest of the report. Here all the unfamiliar terms should be clarified and the concepts of the research problems defined. Some account of what has already been done in this research or problem area should be presented. This section should also explain how the report is organized, so that the reader's mind is programmed accordingly.

10.1.5   Theoretical background

Here the theoretical background to the problem area as well as to the study design is presented. If we are using hypotheses or *a priori* assumptions, there has to be a proper reasoning with the help of previous studies and findings. Depending upon the research orientation, as covered in Chapters 2 and 3, the importance of theory and its use is different. It is therefore important to be consistent in our report and we should check this section with our research orientation and design.

10.1.6   Methodology

In this section we inform the reader of our research design, whether it is exploratory, descriptive or causal, and why a particular design is chosen. We should state the design requirements and how they are met. Different research designs require different methods, as explained in Chapter 4. The research designs, exploratory, descriptive or causal, would also suggest whether we should use qualitative or quantitative methods for our data collection and analysis. This then influences the structure of our report.

We should also inform the reader about our primary and secondary sources of data along with arguments and justifications. When discussing the primary sources, we should explain how we collected information and discuss our population and sampling, and in the case of in-depth case studies, how the cases were selected and why. When writing about data collection, we have to explain what we have done, how we did it and why we have used this particular method.

We should also explain which methods of data analysis have been used: if statistical methods, why these particular methods; if qualitative methods, then how we operationalized different concepts, from where the models came, and what types of conclusion could be drawn through this type of analysis.

10.1.7 Findings

The empirical study, what we have found out from our data collection, is presented here. This section is often a major part of the report as the findings are presented in detail with supportive tables and figures. Here we have to refer back to our research questions or hypotheses and present our findings in accordance with these in a systematic, structured and logical manner. The findings, tables and figures should follow a systematic, chronological or psychological order. The most important job is to sort out irrelevant information and findings.

How to arrange and present the findings of our study is a difficult issue. There are no rules for this, but we should refer to the purpose of the study and the report when it comes to what we want to communicate and to whom. We suggest that researchers should be systematic and choose one of the following methods of presentation:

- *By order of occurrence*. Here you present the findings chronologically. This is particularly suitable when you are working with case studies, or when you have a process or longitudinal approach: for example, when explaining the process of negotiations and factors influencing this process (see, for example, Ghauri, 1983).
- *By criteria or topics*. You may use your own headings — for example, from the questionnaire or problem statement — as a format to present the findings. You may have some criteria on what affects what — for example, independent and dependent variables — which can be used as headings to present the findings. You might number your research questions or hypotheses as 1, 2, 3 . . . and then discuss each of these in the same sequence.
- *By order of location*. You can present your findings from different parts of the country or world in different sections and use these as headings: for example, findings from the south, east or central parts of the country, or findings from different countries or continents.

- *By order of importance*. Quite often it is advised that you present findings in order of importance. The most important and interesting findings should be presented first, followed by the less important issues. When listing criteria, you can list them according to their importance.

10.1.8   Conclusions and recommendations

In this section evaluated facts are discussed, but these evaluations should only be made from the data presented in the earlier sections; the author's biases and desires should not influence these conclusions. You should state your conclusions systematically for each study objective, research question or hypothesis. The best way is to refer back to the objectives or research questions and check whether or not you have provided conclusions for each of these. If the data collected and the analysis do not provide enough information or support to draw conclusions, you should clearly state that. It is important to be specific and concise. We suggest the following format for conclusions:

> *Conclusions:*
> 'Based on our findings our conclusions are: . . .'
> or
> 'We have found that: . . .'

Recommendations for future research or implications for business executives should be based on the findings and conclusions. There should be a logical congruence between conclusions and implications or recommendations. If recommendations or implications are given throughout the report — for example, while presenting findings — these should be summarized and highlighted in this section. We suggest the following format:

> *Implications:*
> 'The implication(s) of C1 is/are: . . .'

10.1.9   Footnotes

As mentioned earlier, the value of a report also depends upon argumentation and sources. Proper credit to these sources is given in two ways: the bibliography or references listed at the end, and the footnotes or references stated throughout the paper. The footnotes specifically and individually document the facts and opinions referred to in the report (Berry, 1989).

In most reports and theses, footnotes are used primarily for three reasons:

- To give credit to the source or earlier study we have used.

- To direct the reader to another section of the same report, also referred to as cross-reference.
- To explain, discuss or provide additional information on a particular concept or issue.

In research reports, a separate reference list or bibliography is provided. In that case we only need to mention the surname of the author and year of publication or source as footnotes: for example, 'Grønhaug (1985)'. These references may also be bracketed within the text at the appropriate point, as in this book.

The type of information that should be documented is a difficult question. A fact that a reader already knows need not be documented: for example, the year when the Second World War ended. However, facts which are not common knowledge have to be documented because we have to inform the reader how we arrived at these facts. It is also important for the sake of intersubjectivity. For example, the result of a study on the buying behaviour of a certain segment needs to be documented with the year of the study because the buying behaviour might change at different times. The behaviour can change due to awareness about environmental pollution, oil crises or any other major incident. Whenever we bring in and use a paraphrase or quotation from another source, it has to be documented with a footnote, together with the page number in the book. This goes for articles or any other source we have used: for example, 'Grønhaug (1985: 18)'.

There are several forms of footnote. One form is to use a single numeral typed as a superscript at the end of the quotation or information to be documented. The same numeral is then repeated at the bottom of the page or at the end of the report, with the source or explanation. Where the footnotes are given at the bottom of the page, they are normally numbered consecutively 1, 2, 3, etc. and new numbers are allotted for the next page starting again with 1. When footnotes are gathered at the end of the report, consecutive numbers are used for all the footnotes in the report. Even for page-to-page footnotes, one can use consecutive numbers for the whole report.

The most important rule is to use the same method throughout the report: different forms should not be mixed up in the same report. When using the form where footnotes are presented at the end of the report, these should come before the list of references or bibliography. Some authors advise using different forms for different types of footnote: for example, footnotes where we only want to document and mention the source might be gathered at the end, while footnotes where we need to explain or discuss a concept might be mentioned at the bottom of the page (Berry, 1989). It is advised that one consistent method should be used for all types of footnote.

There should also be internal consistency. For example, if footnotes are given at the bottom of the page, they should be consistently separated from the main text with double spacing (double the spacing in the text). The footnotes themselves should be in single spacing, while a double space should be given between two footnotes. The margins and numbers should also be consistently at the same place, not only on the same page but throughout the report. For cross-referenced footnotes or references to other parts of the same report, you should avoid referring to later pages, as the reader is not yet aware of what is coming. On the other hand, it is permissible to refer to previous pages: for example, 'see item 2, p. 10'.

10.1.10   Bibliography or references

Bibliographies are lists of books (and other material) on a particular subject and should include *at least* all the sources that have been cited in the report. A list of references, on the other hand, includes *only* those sources cited and should not include books and other material not cited in the report. Bibliographies and reference lists should be in alphabetical order with authors' surnames coming first. If there is no author, the issuing organization's name should come first in the alphabetical order: for example, the European Commission or, in the case of an *editorial* in a periodical, *The Economist*. In the case of a reference to an *article* in a periodical, the author's name should come first.

The most popular format is to place the first word of the first line (e.g. surname) at the left-hand margin, while the rest of the lines are indented by several spaces. Remember, however, that for footnotes, especially those at the foot of the page, the opposite system is often used: the first word of the first line is indented, while the rest of the lines start at the left-hand margin. The bibliography or reference list, like footnotes, should be typed in single spacing, while giving double spacing between two references. Where there is more than one author of a source, it is possible to reverse the names of all authors. However, it is quite common just to reverse the first author's name for the sake of alphabetical order and to mention the rest of the authors with their first name first. Both systems are correct, but for the sake of consistency one should use only one system in the same report.

The titles of books, names of journals, periodicals and newspapers, and titles of published government reports are often underlined, italicized or typed with capital letters. In the case of edited books, if the references come from a chapter written by another author, the reference should start with the author's name and not with the editor's name, and the title of the edited volume or book should be underlined or italicized. The title of articles and chapters from edited books and journals should be indicated by quotation marks (' ') and be typed exactly as the original. If it is in a different language, such as Dutch or Norwegian, it should be cited in the original language. Some common examples of references are provided here:

Dunning, John H. (1980) 'Towards an eclectic theory of international production: some empirical tests', *Journal of International Business Studies*, Spring/Summer, vol. 1, pp. 9–31.

Dunning, John H. (1981) 'Alternative channels and modes of international resource transmission', in Tagi Saagafi-nejad, Richard Moxon and Howard Permutter (eds.), *Controlling International Technology Transfer: Issues, perspectives and implications*, New York: Pergamon.

Kujawa, Duane (ed.) (1975) *International Labor and the Multinational Enterprise*, New York: Praeger.

Robbins, Steve, and Stobaugh, Robert (1973) 'The bent measuring stick for foreign subsidiaries', *Harvard Business Review*, September–October, pp. 80–8.

Stonehill, Arthur, Remmers, Lee, Beekhuisen, Thomas, and Wright, Richard (1975) 'Financial goals in debt ratio determinants: a survey of practice in five countries', *Financial Management*, Autumn, pp. 24–41.

Stopford, John M., and Wells, Luis T., Jr (1972) *Managing the Multinational Enterprise*, New York: Basic Books.

United Nations Center on Transnational Corporations (1985) *International Accounting and Reporting Issues: 1984 review*, New York: United Nations Publications.

As mentioned earlier, there are a number of methods and styles which are correct in listing the bibliography. The most important thing is to use one form throughout a report and not mix up different styles.

10.2   Form and style

The question of form and style is often more a matter of likes and dislikes or individual styles than a matter of rules. However, the following are common mistakes and should be avoided (Grønhaug, 1985):

- *Telegraphic style.* This means that a report is written in sentences without connecting these sentences to each other with any logical consistency.
- *Long and complicated sentences.* Reports are sometimes written in long sentences which are not understandable unless we read them several times. Some students also have a tendency to use difficult and complicated words. Writing short and concise sentences is, however, a good way of writing reports.
- *Usage of terminology and differences between spoken and written language.* When using textbooks or other terminology, you should be sure that the reader understands the usage in the same way. It is quite common for students to use a spoken language form in their report. In report writing you should follow the rules of writing and avoid using the spoken or slang version.
- *Shortage of tables, figures or other illustrations.* You should try to simplify, highlight and complement the important and interesting parts of the report in figures and tables or other illustrations. It is important to point out that these tables and figures should not replace the text. They are used to complement or further explain the text or the point being made.

Our experience as researchers is that we have to write and rewrite reports at least four to five times before they are in a final shape. This version is the working draft, after which you should go through the material once again, along with the data and findings, to see if there is something which has been missed and which should be included in the report. Then read the draft again and start correcting it as you read. Add the information you think is missing and delete the information you feel is irrelevant. At the same time, check that information is correctly placed; if it is not, reshuffle the text. This process should be repeated three or four times. Finally, you should check the language and ideally have someone else read the report. It is quite common, after reading and re-reading the report several times, for you to become blind to drawbacks or mistakes.

   The appearance is very important. It does not matter how well written a report is if it does not look good; it leaves a bad impression on the reader. Here the title page, the quality of typing, margins and the structure of the report are very important. It is easier to read double-spaced reports than single-spaced ones. It is a common practice to use double spacing and indent the first word of each paragraph. In the case of single-spaced reports, double spacing should be used between each paragraph. Regardless of whether the report is single-spaced or double-spaced, the following documents should always be written in single spacing: letters, displayed quotations, footnotes (but use double spacing between them), tables and figures (Murphy and Hildebrandt, 1988).

10.3 Headings

The headings serve as the outline of the report and should be clear, meaningful and consistent. We often number headings to highlight different heading levels, but numbers are not necessary. It is possible to use different styles of type to make these levels explicit. One way is to use the heading style used in this book. The most important aspect is not to use too many levels of heading, as the reader should be able to differentiate easily between different levels of heading and subheading.

10.4 Language and flow

In our opinion, the fewer the words, the better the report. Several short sentences are better than a long sentence. Do not torture the reader by explaining your difficulties in collecting data or interviewing prominent business executives; just tell us what you have done and how you have collected your data. If you are using a concept to explain a certain situation, use the same concept every time you want to explain that situation. In verbal language, when we explain a situation we repeat facts and stories to make sure that the listener has heard and understood what we mean. This is not necessary in written language and you should always avoid repeating things. Reports and theses are never judged according to their length or weight.

As stated previously, people have a tendency to use difficult words and terminology to impress the reader. We strongly recommend using a simple terminology and easily understandable words. Always keep the reader in mind. The business executive who is expected to benefit from the project report might not be aware of the textbook or other professional terminology. In the final report, always use complete sentences; they should have at least one subject and one predicate and should stand alone as having a complete meaning.

When starting a new subject or a new issue or aspect, use a new paragraph. Normally, we do not start a sentence or a paragraph with 'But', 'Because' or a number. If it is necessary to start a sentence with a number, it should be expressed in words: for example, 'Fifty per cent' instead of '50 per cent'. Whatever rules are used, the most important aspect is to be consistent in writing, spelling (for example, UK versus US English), terminology, usage of headings, and figures and tables.

The report, especially the descriptive part, should be written in the first person. Some people believe that impersonal language presupposes objectivity and suggest writing in the third person. We, however, advise that the third-person observer/researcher be charged with 'I' and 'participants' or 'respondents', etc. be charged with 'we' or 'they'.

References

Becker, H.S. (1970) *Sociological Work*, Chicago: Aldine.

Bem, J. (1979) *Désir et savoir dans l'oeuvre de Flaubert: étude de 'La tentation de Saint Antoine'*, Lyon: La Bacconniere.

Bennett, R. (1986) 'Meaning and method in management research', *Graduate Management Research*, vol. 3, no. 3 (whole part).

Berry, R. (1989) *How to Write a Research Paper*, 2nd edn, Oxford: Pergamon.

Beza, T. (1984) *Psaumes mis en vers Français [1551–1562]*, Geneva: Droz.

Bolsky, M.I. (1988) *Better Scientific and Technical Writing*, Englewood Cliffs: Prentice Hall.

Boyd, W.B., and Westfall, R. (1970) 'Interviewer bias once more revisited', *Journal of Marketing Research*, vol. 7, pp. 249–74.

Bradley, M.F. (1987) 'Nature and significance of international marketing: a review', *Journal of Business Research*, vol. 15, pp. 205–19.

Buckley, P.J. (1983) *The Growth of International Business*, London: Allen and Unwin.

Campbell, D.T. (1975) 'Degrees of freedom and the case study', *Comparative Political Studies*, vol. 8, no. 2, pp. 173–93.

Campbell, D.T., and Fiske, W. (1959) 'Convergent and discriminant validation by the multitrail–multimethod matrix', *Psychological Bulletin*, vol. 56, pp. 81–105.

Cannell, C.F., Miller, P.U., and Oksenberg, L. (1981) 'Research on interviewing techniques', in Samuel Leinhardt (ed.), *Sociological Methodology*, San Francisco: Jossey-Bass.

Chalmers, A.F. (1982) *What is this Thing called Science?*, 2nd edn, Philadelphia: Open University Press.

Churchill, G.A. (1979) 'A paradigm for developing better measures of marketing constructs', *Journal of Marketing Research*, vol. 16, February, pp. 64–73.

Churchill, G.A. (1991) *Marketing Research: Methodological foundations*, 5th edn, Chicago: Dryden Press.

Cochran, W.G. (1977) *Sampling Techniques*, 3rd edn, New York: John Wiley and Sons.

Colley, R.H. (1961) *Defining Advertising Goals for Measured Advertising Results*, New York: American Advertising Association.

Cook, T.D., and Campbell, D.T. (1979) *Quasi Experimentation: Design and analysis issues for field settings*, Chicago: Rand McNally College Publication Co.

Cooper, H.M. (1984) *The Integrative Research Review: A systematic approach*, Beverly Hills: Sage.

Douglas, J. (1976) *Investigating Social Research*, Beverly Hills: Sage.

Eisenhardt, K.M. (1989) 'Building theories from case study research', *Academy of Management Review*, vol. 14, no. 4, pp. 532–50.

Fowler, F.J., and Mangione, T.W. (1990) *Standardized Survey Interviewing: Minimizing interviewer-related error*, Newbury Park: Sage.

Frankfort-Nachmias, C., and Nachmias, D. (1992) *Research Methods in Social Sciences*, 4th edn, London: Edward Arnold.

Ghauri, P.N. (1983) *Negotiating International Package Deals*, Stockholm: Almqvist and Wiksell.

Gill, J., and Johnson, P. (1991) *Research Methods for Managers*, London: Paul Chapman.

Glaser, B.G., and Strauss, A.L. (1967) *The Discovery of Grounded Theory: Strategies for qualitative research*, Chicago: Aldine.

Grønhaug, K. (1985) 'Problemer i empirisk forskning', in NHH/RSF, *Methoder og perspectiver i okonomisk-administrativ Forskning*, Oslo: Universitetsforlag.

Grønhaug, K., and Haukedal, W. (1989) 'Environmental imagery and strategic action', *Scandinavian Journal of Management*, vol. 4, no. 1/2, pp. 5–17.

Gujarati, D.N. (1988) *Basic Econometrics*, New York: McGraw-Hill.

Hair, J.F. (1992) *Multivariate Data Analysis*, 3rd edn, New York: Macmillan.

Hawkins, S.W. (1988) *A Brief History of Time: From the big bang to black holes*, Toronto: Bantam Bodes.

Huff, D. (1954) *How to Lie with Statistics*, New York: Norton.

Jankowicz, A.D. (1991) *Business Research Projects for Students*, London: Chapman and Hall.

Johnson, R.A., and Wichern, D.W. (1992) *Applied Multivariate Statistical Analysis*, 3rd edn, Englewood Cliffs: Prentice Hall.

Jones, M.O. (1988) 'In search of meaning: using qualitative methods in research and applications', in M.O. Jones, M.D. Moore and R.C. Snyder (eds.), *Inside Organisations: Understanding the Human Dimension*, London: Sage.

Kent, R.K. (1989) *Marketing Research in Action*, London: Routledge.

Kirk, J., and Miller, M.L. (1986) *Reliability and Validity in Qualitative Research*, New York: Holt, Rinehart and Winston.

Kornhauser, A., and Lazarsfeld, P.F. (1955) 'The analysis of consumer actions', in P.F. Lazarsfeld and M. Rosenberg (eds.), *The Language of Social Research*, Glencoe, Ill.: The Free Press.

Kotler, P. (1991) *Marketing Management*, 7th edn, Englewood Cliffs: Prentice Hall.

Lave, C.A., and March, J.G. (1975) *An Introduction to Models in the Social Sciences*, New York: Harper and Row.

Lazarsfeld, P.E. (1959) 'Latent structure analysis', in S. Koch (ed.), *Psychology: A Study of Science*, vol. III, New York: McGraw-Hill.

Light, D., Jr (1979) 'Surface data and deep structure: observing the organisation of professional training', in J. van Maanen (ed.), *Qualitative Methodology*, Beverly Hills: Sage.

Lofland, J. (1971) *Analyzing Social Settings*, Belmont, CA: Wadsworth.

Maanen, J. van (ed.) (1983) *Qualitative Methodology*, Beverly Hills: Sage.

McGrath, J.E. (1982) 'Dilemmatics: the study of research choices and dilemmas', in J.E. McGrath and R.A. Kulka (eds.), *Independent Calls in Research*, Beverly Hills: Sage.

Martin, C. (1988) *Computers and Senior Managers: Top Management's Response to Interactive Computing*, Manchester: NCC.

Meer-Kooistra, J. v.d. (1993) *Coordineren, Motiveren en verrekenen, Wisselwerking tussen omgeving, onderneming en mensen*, Groningen: Wolters-Noordhoff.

Miles, M.B. (1979) 'Qualitative data as an attractive nuisance: the problem of analysis', in J. van Maanen (ed.), *Qualitative Methodology*, Beverly Hills: Sage.

Miles, M.B., and Huberman, A.M. (1984) *Qualitative Data Analysis: A sourcebook of new methods*, Beverly Hills: Sage.

Mills, J.S. (1961) *A System of Logic*, London: Longman.

Minitab Inc. (1993) *Minitab Reference Manual*, Release 9 for Windows, Lebanon, PA: Minitab Inc.

Mintzberg, H. (1973) *The Nature of Management Work*, New York: Harper and Row.

Mintzberg, H. (1979) 'An emerging strategy of "direct" research', in J. van Maanen (ed.), *Qualitative Methodology*, Beverly Hills: Sage.

Mishler, E.G. (1986) *Research Interviewing*, London: Harvard University Press.

Moser, B., and Kalton, G. (1971) *Survey Methods and Social Investigation*, London: Heinemann.

Murphy, H.A., and Hildebrandt, H.W. (1988) *Effective Business Communications*, 5th edn, New York: McGraw-Hill.

Naegel, E. (1961) *The Structure of Science*, New York: Harcourt, Brace and World.

Norusis, J.M. (1990) *SPSS/PC+ Advanced Statistics 4.0 for the IBM PC/XT/AT and PS/2*, Chicago: SPSS Inc.

Orbell, J. (1987) *A Guide to Tracing the History of a Business*, Aldershot: Gower.

Peters, T.J., and Waterman, R.H. (1982) *In Search of Excellence: Lessons from America's best run company*, New York: Harper and Row.

Popper, K.R. (1961) *The Logic of Scientific Discovery*, New York: Science Edition.

Porter, M.E. (1980) *Competitive Strategy*, New York: The Free Press.

Reeves, T.K., and Harper, D. (1981) *Surveys at Work: A practitioner's guide*, London: McGraw-Hill.

Reichardt, C.S., and Cook, T.D. (1979) 'Beyond qualitative versus quantitative methods', in T.D. Cook and C.S. Reichardt (eds.), *Quantitative Methods in Evaluation Research*, Beverly Hills: Sage.

Revans, R.W. (1971) *Developing Effective Managers*, London: Longman.

SAS Institute Inc. (1988) *SAS/STAT User's Guide*, Release 6.03 Edition, Cary, NC: SAS Institute Inc.

Scheaffer, R.L., Mendenhall, W., and Ott, L. (1990) *Elementary Survey Sampling*, 4th edn, Boston, Mass.: PWS-Kent.

Schumann, H., and Presser, S. (1976) *Questions and Answers in Attitude Surveys: Experiments on question form, wording and context*, New York: Academic Press.

Scott, C. (1961) 'Research on mail surveys', *Journal of the Royal Statistical Society*, vol. 24, no. 124, pp. 143−205.

Selltiz, C., Wrightsman, S., and Cook, S.W. (1976) *Research Methods in Social Relations*, 3rd edn, New York: Holt, Rinehart and Winston.

Simons, R. (1987) 'Accounting control systems and business strategy: an empirical analysis', *Accounting, Organisation and Society*, vol. 12, no. 4, pp. 357−74.

Strauss, A., and Corbin, J. (1990) *Basics of Qualitative Research Grounded Theory Procedures and Techniques*, Newbury Park: Sage.

Sudman, S. (1976) *Applied Sampling*, New York: Academic Press.

Sudman, S., and Bradburn, N.M. (1989) *Asking Questions*, San Francisco: Jossey-Bass.

Weiss, R.S. (1968) 'Issues in holistic research', in H.S. Becker, G. Blanche and R.S. Weiss (eds.), *Institutions and the Person*, Chicago: Aldine.

Whitley, R. (1984) 'The scientific status of management research as a practically oriented social science', *Journal of Management Studies*, 21(4): 369−90.

Yin, R.K. (1984) *Case Study Research: Design and methods*, London: Sage.

Yin, R.K. (1989) *Case Study Research: Design and methods*, 2nd edn, London: Sage.

Zaltman, G., Lemasters, K., and Heffering, M. (1982) *Theory Construction in Marketing*, New York: John Wiley and Sons.

Zaltman, G., Pinson, C.R.A., and Angelmar, R. (1977) *Metatheory and Consumer Research*, New York: Holt, Rinehart and Winston.

Appendix A: Review of statistics

Statistics are an important research tool. In this appendix we have provided the students with a summary of some essentials of the field.

A.1 Basic terms

A unit is a concrete or abstract object or situation of interest to the researcher. Research results are always intended to be valid for some collection of units called a *population*. The *population size* is the number of units in the whole population. It is denoted by N if it is *finite* and by ∞ if it is considered *infinite*. A *value* is a piece of information regarding a particular aspect of the units. A *variable* is a set of values related to a population so that each unit has one and only one value from the set. The values of a *numerical variable* are figures. The values of a *non-numerical variable* cannot immediately be given as figures.

A value of a variable is a characteristic or *an attribute* of some units or *an event* related to some units. A probability is always related to a population. *The probability of an attribute A in a finite population L* is denoted by P(A|L) or usually only by P(A). This probability is the proportion of the units in the population which possess the attribute A.[1] A probability is thus always a proper fraction or 0 or 1 and can be referred to as a *population proportion*. It follows that *the sum of the probabilities of the various values a variable can assume is equal to one*. These values are also called *mutually exclusive events*, since only one of them can be related to a given unit. If there are only two mutually exclusive events related to a variable, these are also called *opposite events* or *complements*. Probability laws and probability calculations are often pretty obvious if one keeps in mind that a probability is a fraction.

144

A.2 Probability distributions

A random variable is a numerical variable related to a population of units. The values of a random variable vary in a more or less random fashion from unit to unit in the population. A random variable is often denoted by a boldface letter or a capital letter. We use an underlined letter, usually $\underline{x}$. The values a random variable can possibly assume can be graphed on a line. The possible values of a *discrete random variable* are points spread on the line with intervals of space between. The possible values of a *continuous random variable* make up a continuous interval on the line.

If the value of the random variable $\underline{x}$ is equal to x for some unit, we say that the random variable $\underline{x}$ *assumes the value x* for that unit. *The probability that x assumes the value x for a random unit* is written $P(\underline{x} = x)$, where $P(\underline{x} = x)$ is the proportion of the units with the value x in the whole population.

The probability function $f(x)$ of a *discrete* random variable, $\underline{x}$, is a mathematical function of the possible values of $\underline{x}$. This function expresses the probabilities of the various values and can thus be written $f(x) = P(\underline{x} = x)$. The probability function is also a *model* and describes the *probability distribution* of the discrete random variable. It tells how frequent the various values of $\underline{x}$ are in the population. Typically, such a model is hypothetical and also approximate. We seldom know beforehand that a particular probability function works. The validity of a particular functional form is often subject to testing.

A probability function must satisfy two mathematical requirements: (1) we must have $0 \leq f(x) \leq 1$ for all values x of $\underline{x}$; (2) the sum of $f(x)$ must be equal to 1 when we sum over all possible values, x of $\underline{x}$. Very many functions fulfil these requirements. Another important question is whether a given probability function actually gives an adequate description of that part of reality which is to be represented by the random variable.

In practice, we have many probability functions available as possible models of a random variable. A handful or so of these functions have proved to be particularly useful. Among these are the *binomial* probability function, the *hypergeometric* probability function and *Poisson's* probability function. Under certain circumstances, these functions can be proven to be appropriate models.

While *discrete* random variables have probability functions, *continuous* random variables have probability *density* functions, often simply called densities. The two kinds of function serve the same purpose, namely to describe the probability distribution of the random variable in question. As a common designation we can therefore use the term *probability distribution* or *distribution*. Although the two kinds of function are used for the same purpose and most often are denoted by the same symbols, they are mathematically quite different.

The *density $f(x)$* of a *continuous* random variable $\underline{x}$ is a mathematical function of x whose graph is a continuous curve stretching above the interval of the x-axis where values of $\underline{x}$ can occur. This function has three important properties: (1) the function is non-negative in the relevant interval and is defined to be 0 elsewhere; (2) the total area between the graph and the x-axis is equal to 1; and (3) the probability that x will assume a value within any interval of any length is equal to the area above that interval and below the corresponding part of the graph of $f(x)$.

Notice the great difference between $f(x)$ in a probability function where it is equal to the probability $P(\underline{x} = x)$ and in a probability *density* function where $f(x)$ is simply the ordinate of x. With a continuous random variable, it is of little interest to ask for the probability of a particular value like $P(\underline{x} = 15)$. *The probability of a particular value of a continuous random variable is always equal to zero.* This may sound strange, but it is exactly true.

The normal probability density function has a bell-shaped graph extending over all of the x-axis from minus infinity to infinity. Theoretical considerations, as well as practical experience, indicate that many random variables in the real world have distributions that can be approximated, relatively closely, by this important distribution. Other important probability density functions are the *Student's t-distribution*, the *F-distribution* and the *chi-square distribution*.

A.3   Descriptive measures in the population

If the *distribution* of a random variable is known, all relevant information regarding that random variable is, in principle, available. Very often, however, it is desirable to summarize this information in various ways. The *population mean* or *expected value* of $\underline{x}$ is denoted by μ or $E(\underline{x})$ and *is simply the average of the values of the random variable for all units in the whole population.* Another important measure of location is the population median. If the values of the random variable for all units in the population have been ordered according to magnitude, the *population median* can be defined as the middle value, or as the average of the two middle values. A similar definition says that *the probability of a value greater than the population median is 0.5.* The *population mode* is in principle defined as the value occurring most often in the population, i.e. the value for which the probability function or the probability density function is a maximum. For a continuous random variable, a vertical line through the population median divides the area below the graph of the probability density function into two equal parts, each of size 0.5. Some densities are *symmetric* about a vertical line through the point on the x-axis corresponding to the population median. *For all symmetric distributions the population mean and the population median are equal.*

The *population variance* of $\underline{x}$ is denoted by var$(\underline{x})$ or σ^2 and is simply *the average of* $(x - \mu)^2$ *for all units in the whole population.* Here σ is a Greek 's' (for spread) and is pronounced 'sigma'. It is very important to understand how variation is measured. Suppose there is no variation at all between the values of $\underline{x}$ in the population. Then all the N values of $\underline{x}$ are equal. Since they are equal, they must all be equal to μ. But then all the deviations $(x_i - \mu)$ as well as their squares must be equal to zero. This results in σ^2 being equal to zero. *If there is no variation between the values of x in the population, then the population variance is equal to zero.* Elaborating on this argument, we can show that *as the variation between the values of x in the population increases, the size of σ^2 also increases.* Another important measure of variation is the *population standard deviation*, σ, which is simply the square root of the population variance.

A.4 Joint distributions and related concepts

The theoretical basis of the important concepts covariance, correlation coefficient and regression function is the joint distribution of the random variables in question. *The joint probability function f(x, y) of two discrete random variables, $\underline{x}$ and $\underline{y}$, is a function of the* possible values of the two random variables. This function expresses the probabilities of the various combinations of values and can thus be written $f(x, y) = P[(\underline{x} = x) \cap (\underline{y} = y)]$, where x and y represent arbitrary values that we are allowed to specify. The symbol $\cap$ is an *intersection* symbol and can be read 'both . . . and . . .'.

In applications there is frequently an *association* between the values of two random variables. In a population of firms, there may, for instance, be an association between $\underline{x}$ = the average number of employees in 1993 and $\underline{y}$ = the profit in 1993. This association or correlation could be *positive* if firms with high values of $\underline{x}$ tend to have high values of $\underline{y}$, or it could be *negative* if the relationship is the opposite. *The population covariance* between two random variables $\underline{x}$ and $\underline{y}$ is denoted by $\text{cov}(\underline{x}, \underline{y})$ or σ_{xy}. It is a measure of the relationship between the values of the two random variables in the population. Suppose that, for each unit in the population, we find the product $(x - \mu_x)(y - \mu_y)$. *The population covariance is then simply the population mean of all those products*. In general, $\underline{x}$ and $\underline{y}$ are said to be *uncorrelated, correlated, positively correlated* or *negatively correlated*, depending on whether σ_{xy} is zero, different from zero, positive or negative. A measure closely related to the population covariance is the population correlation coefficient ρ (Greek small 'r', pronounced 'rho'). *The population correlation coefficient ρ_{xy} between* two random variables $\underline{x}$ and $\underline{y}$ is obtained by dividing the covariance by the product of the population standard deviations of the two random variables.

The properties of ρ_{xy} are similar to those of σ_{xy}, except that *the value of ρ_{xy} always lies between -1 (complete negative correlation) and 1 (complete positive correlation)*. If one of the two coefficients is zero, the other is also zero. The signs are also equal.

A.5 Independence

A very important concept related to correlation is the concept of independence. *Two events or attributes, A and B, are independent if and only if the joint probability of the two* is equal to the product of the marginal probabilities, i.e. if $P(A \cap B) = P(A)P(B)$.

Two random variables $\underline{x}$ and $\underline{y}$ are independent if and only if the joint probability distribution of the two is equal to the product of the two marginal probability distributions. A *marginal probability distribution* here means a usual probability distribution for only one variable. A useful rule says: *if two random variables are independent, then they are also uncorrelated*. The opposite is not always true, but it is true if the two random variables are normally distributed. The conditions for independence can also be stated in terms of conditional distributions, but we do not pursue this here.

If the expected value of $\underline{y}$ in the conditional distribution is expressed as a function of the condition x, we get the population regression function of $\underline{y}$ on x. $\underline{y}$ or y is then called the *dependent variable* and $\underline{x}$ or x is called the *independent variable*. Whatever symbols are used, the independent variable is usually graphed on the x-axis and the dependent variable on the y-axis. With one independent variable we deal with *simple regression* and, if the regression function considered is linear, we have *linear regression*. Regression functions need not be linear. If the expected value of one random variable can be expressed as a non-linear function of the values of another random variable, we talk about a *curvilinear population regression function*.

It is possible to imagine a situation where the expected value of one random variable, say $\underline{y}$, is a linear function of the values of several other random variables, $\underline{x}_1$, $\underline{x}_2$, $\underline{x}_3$, . . ., $\underline{x}_k$. Here, $\underline{y}$ could be profit, $\underline{x}_1$ could be employees, $\underline{x}_2$ accumulated investments, $\underline{x}_3$ advertising expenditures, and so on. *The multiple linear population regression function* of $\underline{y}$ on $\underline{x}_1$, $\underline{x}_2$, $\underline{x}_3$, . . ., $\underline{x}_k$ can be written as shown in (A.1).

$$E(\underline{x}_2 | x_1 x_2 \ldots x_k) = \beta_0 + \beta_1 x_1 + \beta_2 x_2 + \ldots + \beta_k x_k \tag{A.1}$$

Here, β_0 is the constant term and β_1 is the *partial population regression coefficient* of $\underline{y}$ on $\underline{x}_1$ or x_1. The other βs would be denoted in a similar fashion. The concept of a regression function can be used even if the x-es on the right-hand side of the equals sign are not values of random variables, but just chosen constants. This could be the case in an experimental situation where the chosen constants are experimental conditions.

The *multiple population correlation coefficient* P (Greek capital 'R', pronounced 'rho') is a useful measure in connection with multiple regression. Its role is similar to ρ, the simple population correlation coefficient. One difference is that P can never be negative; its value is always a figure between 0 and 1. If P $= 0$, there is no linear relationship between the independent variables and the dependent variable. If P $= 1$, the dependent variable is an exact linear function of the independent variables.

A.6   Models, parameters and assumptions

So far in this appendix, we have described the basic statistical concepts *related to a population*. In the present section, we intend to give an overview of the use of these concepts in a larger statistical context.

Statistics is a discipline where one works with theoretical models of the real world. *A probability distribution is a model for that part of reality represented by the random variable(s) of the problem*. One of the most basic tasks when dealing with a statistical problem is to choose an appropriate model. As mentioned earlier, there is, in principle, an infinite number of models to choose from. But theoretical considerations, practical experience and the necessity of choosing a model which is mathematically handy have led to certain models that are used again and again in the literature. A few of the most useful models are mentioned briefly below.

Most models of general interest have one or more parameters. From the point of view of statistical theory, *a parameter* can be defined as a constant found in the (joint) probability distribution of the random variable(s) under study. Further, this constant is such that it may have different values in different applications or in different populations.

From the practical, or application, point of view, *a parameter* can be defined as a constant describing a certain part of reality. A parameter can be the *population mean* of a certain random variable. It is important to realize that statistics is a complicated field where models are not necessarily of the relatively simple kind implied so far. There are also 'systems of models' at a higher level of thought, so to say. We can, for instance, study a model (system) where one random variable is a function of several other random variables. In such cases, a parameter can be the difference between two population means, the difference between two population proportions, or other similar or more complicated functions of basic population constants.

The normal density, mentioned before, has *two parameters*, namely the population mean, μ, and the population standard deviation, σ, of the random variable $\underline{x}$ we are considering. The graph of this density is symmetric around a vertical line through the point μ on the x-axis and stretches above all of the x-axis. The function has its maximum where $x = \mu$. The distance from μ to the inflection point of the graph on either side of μ can be shown to be equal to σ. It is very difficult, if not impossible, to find a real-life random variable which can have values from $-\infty$ to ∞. The normal model is therefore usually not more than an *approximation* to the true probability density function. But the approximation is often surprisingly good. If we are to describe the distribution of a real-life random variable by means of the normal density function, appropriate values of μ and σ must be chosen. The size of μ determines where the 'bell' is located on the x-axis. The size of σ determines the 'concentration' of the area of the 'bell' around μ.

We shall briefly mention various joint distributions. If $\underline{x}$ is normally distributed with parameters equal to μ and σ, we will use the *notation* '$\underline{x}$ is $N(\mu, \sigma^2)$' for brevity. Let us consider two random variables, $\underline{x}_1$ and $\underline{x}_2$. We will assume that $\underline{x}_1$ is $N(\mu_1, \sigma_1^2)$ with probability density function $f_1(x_1)$ and that $\underline{x}_2$ is $N(\mu_2, \sigma_2^2)$ with probability density function $f_2(x_2)$. If, in addition, we assume that $\underline{x}_1$ and $\underline{x}_2$ are *independent* random variables, then the joint probability density function of $\underline{x}_1$ and $\underline{x}_2$ is given by $f(x_1, x_2) = f_1(x_1)f_2(x_2)$. This density has four parameters, namely μ_1, σ_1, μ_2 and σ_2. The function is a special case of the so-called *bivariate normal probability density function*. In the general case where the two random variables may be correlated, the population covariance σ_{12} between the two is also added to the list of parameters.

The joint distribution of a set of k independent random variables is equal to the product of the k individual distributions. This important fact is often used in formulating models.

The *multivariate normal probability density function* is the basis for many statistical methods. If k random variables follow this distribution, then the parameters consist of k population means, k population standard deviations and $(k^2 - k)/2$ covariances, namely the covariances between all pairs of random variables. If the k random variables follow a multivariate normal distribution, then each marginal and conditional distribution is also some kind of normal distribution.

Mathematically, a variance and a covariance are very similar entities. Notice that the covariance between a random variable and itself is equal to the variance of that random variable. Instead of denoting the variance of, say, $\underline{x}_1$ by σ_1^2, we can just as well use the covariance notation σ_{11}.

A *matrix* is a rectangular or quadratic table of figures included in brackets. The matrix

consists of *rows* and *columns* of figures. The figures are called the *elements* of the matrix.
A *row vector* is a matrix consisting of only one row. A *column vector* is a matrix
consisting of only one column. The parameters of a multivariate normal distribution are
often presented in a *population mean vector* $\mu = [\mu_1, \mu_2, \mu_3 \ldots \mu_k]'$ and a so-called
population variance—covariance matrix or *population dispersion matrix* Σ containing all
the variances and covariances mentioned above.[2] Such a matrix, which is a *square matrix*,
is indicated in a general form in (A.2).

$$
\Sigma = \begin{bmatrix}
\sigma_{11} & \sigma_{12} & \sigma_{13} & \cdot & \cdot & \cdot & \sigma_{1k} \\
\sigma_{21} & \sigma_{22} & \sigma_{23} & \cdot & \cdot & \cdot & \sigma_{2k} \\
\sigma_{31} & \sigma_{32} & \sigma_{33} & \cdot & \cdot & \cdot & \sigma_{3k} \\
\cdot & \cdot & \cdot & \cdot & \cdot & \cdot & \cdot \\
\cdot & \cdot & \cdot & \cdot & \cdot & \cdot & \cdot \\
\cdot & \cdot & \cdot & \cdot & \cdot & \cdot & \cdot \\
\sigma_{k1} & \sigma_{k2} & \sigma_{k3} & \cdot & \cdot & \cdot & \sigma_{kk}
\end{bmatrix} \tag{A.2}
$$

The elements with two equal subscripts in the matrix are the variances. They are located
along what is called the *main diagonal* of the matrix. As explained before, if we divide a
population covariance by the two population standard deviations having the
corresponding subscripts, we get the corresponding population correlation coefficient.
We also remind the reader of the fact that *the correlation coefficient between a variable
and itself is 1*. Performing the divisions described in this paragraph on the elements of the
matrix (A.2), we get the corresponding *population correlation matrix* P, which we have
not shown. Along the main diagonal of this square matrix there are only 1s. If all the other
elements in the population correlation matrix are 0, all the random variables are
uncorrelated. For normally distributed random variables, this means that they are also
independent.

We now turn to the very important topic of *making assumptions* in statistics. First, we
remind the reader of the fact that science or research without assumptions is impossible.
As human beings we always have imperfect knowledge and have to assume something
about the unknown. A very basic assumption in statistics is the assumption regarding the
mathematical form of the joint distribution of the random variables involved in the
problem. The main body of well-established statistical methods is based, in some way,
upon assumptions of normal distributions. Very often certain random variables are also
assumed to be *independent*. This assumption greatly simplifies the analysis. A next
question regards the *numerical values (sizes) of the parameters*. Typically, these are not
subject to assumptions but to statistical inference, which will be treated later.

A.7 Describing the sample

In this section we very briefly mention some sample measures of location and variation, any of which have counterparts in the population. Each sample measure can be regarded as an *estimate* of the corresponding population measure, and the population measure can often be regarded as a *parameter* of some distribution. The random variable (or sometimes the formula) that produces the estimate is often called an *estimator*. Some textbooks do not distinguish clearly between an estimate and an estimator.

In this section we assume that a single random variable, denoted by $\underline{x}$, is of interest. Further, we assume that a random sample of size n has been drawn from the population. The resulting observations of $\underline{x}$ will be denoted by $x_1, x_2, \ldots, x_n$ or also x_j ($j = 1, 2, \ldots, n$). These fresh observations are often called *raw data*.

If we arrange the observations in increasing order of magnitude, the *sample median* is defined as the middle value. If there are two equal values in the middle, the sample median is defined as the arithmetic mean of the two middle values. The *sample mode* is the value that occurs most frequently in the sample (if there is any such value). The mode is especially useful for qualitative data. In a collection of customers from various countries, the *modal* nationality is the nationality that occurs most frequently. For a frequency distribution with classes, we could talk about the *modal class*.

If we are able to find a value having the property that 25 per cent (i.e. one-quarter) of the sample values are smaller than that value, while 75 per cent are larger, that value is called the *first quartile*. Similarly, the *third quartile* is a value so large that 75 per cent of the sample values are smaller. *Deciles* (deci = 10) and *percentiles* are defined similarly. The reader will understand that there are several percentiles, deciles and quartiles. A common name for such a magnitude is *quantile*. The median may be called the second *quartile* or the *50th percentile*. Still another name for the median is the *5th decile*.

Two points should be remembered in connection with the quantiles described above. First, they are all sample magnitudes and therefore we could very well use the word 'sample' to characterize them further, e.g. the first *sample* quartile. The corresponding quantiles in the population are often called *fractiles*. Second, the various quantiles are often computed in a way which is slightly different from our description above. Therefore, the results may also be a little different. Commonly, the quantiles are calculated from a frequency distribution. They can also very conveniently be read off graphically from various diagrams derived from the frequency distribution like a *percentage ogive* or a *cumulative relative frequency polygon*. This method of obtaining quantiles is precise enough for most purposes. The differences in results mentioned are quite unimportant.

The definitions of the sample variance and the sample standard deviation are similar to the definitions of the corresponding population measures. A minor difference is found in the denominator. The denominator of the sample variance is usually $n - 1$, while the denominator of the population variance is N.

A *relative* measure of variation is the *coefficient of variation*, which is the standard deviation as a percentage or fraction of the mean. This measure can also be used both in the sample and in the population. A very simple measure of variation is the *range*, which is equal to the largest value minus the smallest value. There are also measures of variation which are based upon quantiles. The *interquartile range* is equal to the third quartile minus the first quartile. This figure by itself tells something about the variation. More commonly used is the *semi-interquartile range* or *quartile deviation Q*, which is one-half of the interquartile range.

The *sample covariance* $\text{cov}(\underline{x}, \underline{y}) = s_{xy}$ between two random variables $\underline{x}$ and $\underline{y}$ has a formula which is similar to the population formula, but we use sample values and sample size instead of using population values and population size. Notice again that we use $n - 1$ in the denominator.

The *sample correlation coefficient* r_{xy} between $\underline{x}$ and $\underline{y}$ can be computed just like the corresponding population coefficient. The only difference is that the population covariance and the population standard deviations are replaced by the corresponding sample magnitudes. In problems where several variables are involved, the *sample variance – covariance matrix* or *sample dispersion matrix*, S, and the *sample correlation matrix*, R, are often utilized. These matrices are defined just like the corresponding population matrices, except that the elements are sample magnitudes.

A.8 Sampling and sampling distributions

It is important to notice that if we imagine taking repeated samples of the same size, n (we never do that in practice), then $\bar{x}$ will usually be different in different samples. *Thus we can introduce a random variable $\bar{x}$ and regard the various sample means as being values of that random variable.* The random variable $\underline{\bar{x}}$ is called a *sample random variable*, since the units we have to imagine in connection with this random variable are samples. The distribution of this random variable is called a *sampling distribution*.

The properties of the sampling distribution of $\underline{\bar{x}}$ are important for judging the validity and reliability of our estimation procedure. The question of *validity* is the question of whether on average, or in the long run, the mean of all conceivable $\bar{x}$s is equal to μ. If this is the case, we say that $\underline{\bar{x}}$ is an *unbiased estimator* of μ. The question of *reliability* is a question of whether the variance $\text{var}(\underline{\bar{x}})$ of $\underline{\bar{x}}$ is sufficiently small. If it is smaller than for other estimators, it is sometimes said to be *best*. As a matter of fact, $\bar{x}$ really is an unbiased estimator of μ and its variance can be shown to be equal to σ^2/n if the population is infinite. If the population is finite, σ^2/n must be multiplied by the *finite population correction factor*, $(N - n)/(N - 1)$, to yield the variance of $\underline{\bar{x}}$. Similarly, in repeated samples of a constant size, n, we can think of a sample random variable $\underline{s}^2$ whose values are the various figures s^2.

A very important sampling distribution is the *Student's t-distribution*. This probability density has one parameter, called the number of degrees of freedom. The parameter is often denoted by '*d.f.*'. A sample random variable which follows the Student's *t*-distribution can be constructed in various ways for various purposes. The simplest way is shown in (A.3), where the starting point is a random variable $\underline{x}$ which is $N(\mu, \sigma^2)$. We assume that a random sample of n observations of that random variable has been drawn and that x and s have been computed the usual way.

$$t = \frac{x - \mu}{s/\sqrt{n}} \quad \text{or} \quad \underline{t} = \frac{\underline{\bar{x}} - \mu}{s/\sqrt{n}} \qquad d.f. = n - 1$$

$$\text{(A.3)}$$

This sample random variable may be thought of as the same as $\bar{x}$, except that it has been measured in other units, i.e. with μ as the origin and with the estimated standard deviation s/n of $\bar{x}$ as the unit of measurement. The Student's t-distribution is an extremely important tool in statistical inference. Two other distributions play a similar role, namely *Fischer's F-distribution* and the *chi-square or* X^2-*distribution*. ('X' is a Greek 'ch', pronounced 'chi'.) The chi-square distribution has one parameter, called the number of degrees of freedom, and is in this respect similar to the t-distribution. The F-distribution has two parameters called, respectively, the number of degrees of freedom for numerator and the number of degrees of freedom for denominator.[3] To describe the role of these three distributions in statistical inference will bring us too far off the main road. It is sufficient here to say that they are tools used in drawing inferences. In connection with their use, some basic random variables are usually assumed to be *normally distributed*. The number of degrees of freedom is a function of one or more sample sizes, or depends on the number of variables. On the basis of the number of degrees of freedom and some pre-chosen probabilities, fractiles of these distributions are found in tables and used to draw practical conclusions.

A.9   Principles of statistical inference

A.9.1   Introduction

The science of drawing inferences from a sample to a population is called *statistical inference*. It includes *estimation* and *hypothesis testing*. To *estimate* means to assess an unknown population constant on the basis of a corresponding sample magnitude. An example of such an unknown population constant is a *population proportion*: for instance, the proportion of firms having a female president in a population of firms. A commonly used symbol for such a proportion is $P(F) = p$, if 'F' denotes 'female'. This proportion is called the *probability of F*. An *estimate* of this proportion could be the sample proportion $\hat{p} = \hat{P}(F) = x/n$. Here x is the number of firms with a female president in the sample of size n. The corresponding estimator would be $\hat{\underline{p}} = \hat{P}(\underline{A}) = \underline{x}/n$. This estimator can have different values in different samples, since $\underline{x}$ will be a sample random variable with a hypergeometric or binomial distribution. Actually, $\hat{\underline{p}}$ will be approximately normally distributed if n is large ($n \geq 30$).

Let us imagine a large table. The columns contain all variables that are relevant for a particular study. The rows contain values of all those variables for all units in the population. Such a table could be called a *population data matrix*. The purpose of a quantitative business study is normally not to establish or uncover the whole population data matrix. Such a research objective would in most cases be far too ambitious and is only carried out in a so-called *complete census*. *The objective of a study is typically to estimate some population constants that are in some way or another descriptive of the population data matrix.*

Examples of such constants are population means, population proportions or probabilities, population standard deviation or variances, population correlation coefficients, population regression coefficients, and other population parameters of postulated distributions of the variables. Constants of a more derived nature are population elasticities that can be derived from, for example, regression coefficients. Also, in connection with many of the more advanced methods, one can say that the objective of the study is to estimate various population constants. But in some cases the objective is more sophisticated (cluster analysis and multidimensional scaling).

A.9.2   Computing confidence limits

A central concern of estimation is the error of estimation. If the estimate is $\bar{x}$, let us first consider the *error of estimation in estimating μ*. This error is equal to the absolute value of $\bar{x} - \mu$ which is written $|\bar{x} - \mu|$. Very often we attack the estimation problem in the following way. (1) We choose a relatively high probability, say 0.95, and denote this probability by $1 - \alpha$.[4] This probability is called a *confidence probability*. (2) We construct an interval around $\bar{x}$ in such a way that the probability that the interval will contain μ is equal to $1 - \alpha$. This interval is called a *confidence interval*. (3) We take the chance of saying that μ is equal to $\bar{x}$. Then there is a probability of $1 - \alpha$ that the error of estimation will be at most equal to half the width of the confidence interval. The two limits (lower and upper) of a confidence interval are called *confidence limits*. In statistical textbooks you will find formulae for confidence limits for many kinds of unknown constant or for differences between unknown constants.

In general, a confidence interval can be defined as follows: a *confidence interval for an unknown constant* is an interval having the property that there is a certain probability, chosen beforehand and denoted by $1 - \alpha$, that the interval will be located in such a position that it will contain the unknown constant.

The derivation of formulae for confidence limits is based upon the application of sampling distributions like the Student's t-distribution and the chi-square distribution, or the standardized normal distribution. The practical use of these formulae involves the choice of a confidence probability and finding a fractile of the relevant distribution in a table.

A.9.3   Testing hypotheses

A central research activity is the testing of hypotheses. A *hypothesis* is a preliminary assertion regarding some unknown phenomenon. A *statistical hypothesis* is a hypothesis regarding some statistical magnitude (usually a parameter of some distribution), like a probability, a population mean, the difference between two population means, a population regression coefficient, a population standard deviation, etc.

The hypothesis to be tested is often referred to as the *null-hypothesis* and is denoted by H or H_0. When a hypothesis H is set forth, one must also always state the *alternative hypothesis* to H, i.e. the hypothesis we think is true if H is not true. The alternative hypothesis, or simply the *alternative* to H, is often denoted by A, H_A or H_1. The choice of the alternative is always such that either it or the hypothesis must be true. There must be no other possibilities.

To *test* a hypothesis, H, against an alternative hypothesis, A, means confronting the hypothesis with facts derived from observed sample data. On the basis of this confrontation the conclusion is drawn, either to *reject* H as being false, and therefore to accept A, or to *accept* H (at least on a preliminary basis).

Testing is actually performed by considering the distribution of a certain sample random variable called a *test statistic*. The distribution of the test statistic is derived on the assumption that the hypothesis, H, is true. If the value of the test statistic computed on the basis of the actual sample data is found to be extreme (i.e. rare or strange), the hypothesis is rejected. The value is considered extreme if the probability, P, of getting such a value, or an even stranger value, given that H is true, is small. Deciding what to consider extreme is also guided by the choice of the alternative hypothesis. The probability, P, is called the *P-value* or the *tail probability* or the *attained level of significance*.

The P-value is compared with another probability called the *level of significance*, usually denoted by α. *The rule always is that H is rejected if P is smaller than α.* If the purpose of the testing procedure is to arrive at an objective scientific conclusion and decision, the level of significance should logically and ethically be chosen before the data have been examined. Common choices for α are 0.05 (i.e. 5 per cent), 0.01 or 0.1. If the study is of a more descriptive nature, one may present P-values without choosing a level of significance.

The level of significance is the maximum value we are willing to approve regarding the probability of rejecting H, given that H is actually true. The error of rejecting H, given that H is true, is called *type I error* or rejection error. In order to try to avoid that error, α is usually chosen to be small. The error of accepting H, given that A is true, is called *type II error* or acceptance error. The probability of accepting H, given that A is true, is often denoted by β. For a given sample size, the situation in general is that if we decrease α, β is automatically increased. Therefore, we have to make a compromise. In the absence of further criteria, α is often chosen conventionally equal to 0.05, but other figures are also used.

When α has been chosen, the *critical values* of the test statistic, i.e. the limiting values between rejection of H and acceptance of H, can be derived provided the sampling distribution of the test statistic is completely known or can be assumed. Thus a *rejection rule*, describing a *rejection region* containing the values of the test statistic for which the hypothesis H should be rejected, can be stated. Instead of finding critical values of the test statistic, as described in the preceding paragraph, we can use the sampling distribution of the test statistic to determine the P-value of the computed sample value of the test statistic. This P-value can then be compared directly with α, as described earlier.

Suppose we want to test a hypothesis regarding a population mean, μ. The hypothesis may be written H: $\mu = \mu_H$, where μ_H is the hypothetical value. The alternative could possibly be A: $\mu \neq \mu_H$. This is called a *two-sided alternative* because the values of the parameter according to A lie on two sides of the value corresponding to H. We would then reject H if $\bar{x}$ is either very small or very large compared to μ_H. If, for some reason, we know that μ cannot possibly be smaller than μ_H, the alternative to H would be chosen as A: $\mu > \mu_H$. Then we have what is called a *one-sided alternative*.[5] In that case we would reject H only if $\bar{x}$ is large compared to μ_H. Thus, the rejection region will be different, even if α is the same. Another example of a one-sided alternative would be A: $\mu < \mu_H$.

The example above illustrates the general principle of hypothesis testing, but there are also many other kinds of hypothesis and other kinds of test statistics. Instead of using $\bar{x}$ as a test statistic in the example, a Student's t-statistic is more often used, for various reasons. The principle of testing is still the same, however. A t-value can be thought of as an $\bar{x}$ measured in other units. In the t-formula (A.3), we use μ_H for μ to define a test statistic as shown in (A.4).

$$\underline{t_H} = \frac{\bar{x} - \mu_H}{s/\sqrt{n}} \quad \text{or} \quad t_H = \frac{x - \mu_H}{s/\sqrt{n}} \qquad d.f. = n - 1 \tag{A.4}$$

If H is true, the expected value of t_H is equal to 0. If t_H calculated from the sample deviates much from 0, the hypothesis must thus be rejected. When the level of significance and the alternative have been chosen, critical values for t_H can be found from a table showing fractiles of the t-distribution. $\underline{t_H}$ is namely distributed according to the Student's t-distribution if H is true.

Computer programs for testing hypotheses usually present P-values. If the program assumes a two-sided alternative (which is common) and you want to use a one-sided alternative, you can divide the presented P-value by 2.

Notes

1. If the population is infinite, mathematical stringency requires a more elaborate definition, since we are not allowed to divide by infinity. For practical purposes, our definition will work even for infinite populations if we think of such populations as being not infinite, but very large, as they actually are.
2. (a) The prime ' after the mean vector indicates that the corresponding column vector is meant, not a row vector as listed. (b) The Σ in this context stands for the population dispersion matrix and is not the same Σ that was previously used to signify summation.
3. An F can always be thought of as being a fraction.
4. This α has nothing to do with the constant term in the population regression function. The symbol is just used with two different meanings, which is quite common.
5. The name signifies that the values according to the alternative hypothesis are on *one side* of the hypothetical value on the line. In regression analysis, we often test a hypothesis H: $\beta = \beta_H = 0$ (e.g. expected demand is *not related to* price) against a one-sided alternative, A: $\beta < \beta_H = 0$ (expected demand *decreases with* price).

Index

activity guidance model 23
alternative hypothesis 154
analytical surveys 59—60
assumptions in statistics 150

bibliography, final report 137, 138—9
binomial probability function 145
bivariate probability density function 149

canonical correlation analysis 130
case study method 65—6, 87—93
  comparative case studies 88
  conducting 91—2
  preparation 89—90
  selection of cases 90—1
  skills required and training 89—90
  types of case study design 92—3
causal modelling 37
causal research 27, 29
causal studies 90
cause and effect 29—30, 49
chi-square distribution 146, 153
chi-squared test 102, 105
cluster analysis, 128, 129—30
cluster sampling 79—80
  compared with stratified random sampling
    79—80
coding 98
coefficient of variation 151
column vector 150
common factor 128
concepts 17—19
  definition 17
  functions 17
conceptual definitions 18, 51
confidence interval 154

confidence limits, computing 154
confidence probability 154
construct validity 48—9
continuous random variable 145
control groups, reasons for using 32
convergent validity 48
correlation matrix 128
correlational research design 35—7
covariance, sample 152
covariance, population 147
Crohnbach's α 47
cross-sectional designs 35—7
cross-tabulation of data 102—6
cumulative relative frequency polygon 151

data, link with propositions 90
data analysis 97—131
  canonical correlation analysis 130
  cluster analysis 128, 129—30
  cross-tabulation of data 102—6
  dummy variables 118—22
  factor analysis 128—9
  linear discriminant analysis 122—4
  multidimensional scaling (MDS) 130
  multiple regression analysis 114—18
  multivariate analysis 129
  multivariate analysis of variance (MANOVA)
    130—1
  non-parametric methods 101, 107—9
  one variable 99—102
  one-way analysis of variance 109
  principle components analysis 125—8
  sign test 107—8
  simple linear regression 110—14
  statistical software packages 99
  two or more variables *see* data analysis,
    cross-tabulation of data

data analysis (*continued*)
  two sample problems regarding population
    means 106−10
  unpaired observations 108−10
  Wilcoxon signed-rank test 108
  see also regression analysis
data collection 54−72
  primary data *see* separate entry
  secondary data 54−7
data matrix 76 Table, 98
deciles 151
deduction 8−10
  compared with induction 9
  meaning of 8, 9
definitions 18
  properties 18
demand elasticity 75
dependent variable 31, 147
descriptive measures in population 146
descriptive model 21
descriptive studies 90
design errors 27
discrete random variable 145
  probability function 145
divergent validity 48

eigenvalue, definition 126
error of estimation, definition 80
errors of rejection 155
estimation 153
executive summary 132, 134
exhaustive categories 100
explanation model 22
external validity 33, 50

face validity 48
factor analysis 128−9
  comparison with principal components
    analysis 128
final report,
  bibliography 137, 138−9
  conclusions 136
  executive summary 132, 134
  findings 132, 135−6
  footnotes 136−7
  form and style 139−40
  headings 140
  introduction 134
  language and flow 140
  methodology 132, 134−5
  problem statement 134
  recommendations 136

references 138−9
  structure 132−9
  table of contents 133
  theoretical background 134
  title page 133
  writing 132−40
first-stage units *see* cluster sampling
Fischer's F-distribution, description 146, 153
formative measurements 48
fractiles 151

goodness of fit 102
group discussions 86, 87

headings, final report 140
historical reviews 86, 87
homoscedasticity assumption 113
hypergeometric probability function 145
hypothesis, definition 154
hypothesis testing 153, 154−6

in-depth interviews 65−6
  see also case study method
independence, concept of 147−8
independent variable 147−8
  definition 31
induction 8−10
  compared with deduction 9
  meaning of 8, 9 Fig
internal validity 33, 49−50
interquartile range 151
interview guide 66
interviewer(s), choice of 67−8
interviews,
  bias 65
  confidentiality 67
  confirmation appointment letter 68
  contacting proposed interviewee 67
  developing relationship with interviewee 70
  in-depth 65−6
  the interview 69−71
  language used 69
  post-interview 71−2
  preparation 66−8
  recording 67
    on tape or video 67, 71
  semi-structured interviews 64−5
  sensitive questions 70
  social conventions 68−9
  structured 65
  survey research interviews 64

interviews (*continued*)
  thanking respondent 71
  time taken 66−7, 70
  typology 65 Fig
  unstructured interviews 64, 65
  what to wear 68−9

joint distributions and related concepts 147
joint probability function, description 147

Kruskal-Wallis test 109−10

language and flow, final report 140
level of significance 102, 155
  attained 155
linear discriminant analysis 122−4
linear regression 148
linear regression analysis, simple 110−14
LISREL 37
literature review 23−4
loadings 129
logistic regression 122

Mann-Whitney test 108−9
mapping 42, 53
matrix, description 149−50
mean 75, 100
  designation 146
mean, unknown population 100
measurements 41−53
  defining 41−3
  formative 48
  improving 51−2
  indicators 43, 44 Fig
  levels 43−5
    interval 44 Table, 45
    nominal 44−5
    ordinal 44 Table, 45
    ratio scale 44 Table, 45
  mapping 42, 53
  qualitative research 52−3
  reflective 48
  rules 42−3
  summary 44 Table
  validity and reliability 46−50
    construct validity 48−9
    external validity 50
    internal validity 49−50
  multi-trait multi-method approach 48−9
    multiple indicators 47−8
  statistical conclusion validity 50
median 100, 151

methodology 132, 134−5
Minitab 99
mode 146, 151
models 148
models in research 19−23
  activity guidance model 23
  characteristics 20
  descriptive model 21
  explanation model 22
  prediction/forecasting model 22−3
  purposes 20−3
modified *t*-test 108
multidimensional scaling (MDS) 130
multiple case design 93
multiple indicators 47−8
multiple linear population regression function 148
multiple population correlation coefficient 148
multiple regression analysis,
  partial regression coefficients 115
  partial *t*-tests 115
multiple response 98
multivariate analysis 129
multivariate analysis of variance (MANOVA) 130−1
multivariate normal probability density function 149
mutually exclusive categories 100

non-probability sampling 74
normal probability density functions 146
normal probability plot 113
null-hypothesis 154

observations,
  as data collection tool 57−8
  storage 97−8
one-shot case study 37−8
one-sided alternative, descriptive 155−6
open-ended questions 61
operational definitions 18−19, 43, 51
organizational chart 21
orthogonal variables 117

P-value 155
paired observations, data analysis 106−8
parameters,
  definitions 75, 148−9
  examples 75
partial correlation coefficient, formula 40
partial population regression coefficient 148

partial regression coefficients 115
partial *t*-tests 115
path analysis 37
PC analysis *see* principle components analysis
percentage ogive 151
percentiles 151
perfect multicollinearity 117
phenomenological attitude 96
pilot study 66
Poisson's probability function 145
population, definition 144
population census 54
population correlation coefficients 75
population correlation matrix 150
population dispersion matrix 150
population mean vector 150
population regression coefficients 75
population variance-covariance matrix 150
positivistic orientation 96
prediction/forecasting model 22 – 3
primary data 57 – 72
  definition 54, 57
  interviews, 64 – 72
  observations 57 – 8
  surveys and questionnaires 58 – 64
    analytical surveys 59 – 60
    descriptive surveys 60
    guidelines for construction and wording of
      questionnaires 62 – 4
    length of questionnaires 61
    open-ended questions 61
    planning 59 Fig, 60 – 2
primary sampling units *see* cluster sampling
principal components analysis 125 – 8
  comparison with factor analysis 128
probability density functions 145 – 6
  normal 146
probability distributions 145 – 6
probability function,
  binomial 145
  discrete random variable 145
  hypergeometric 145
  Poisson's 145
probability sampling 74
problem representation 19 – 20
problem structure, and research designs 27 – 9
profit planning 22
property-disposition relationships 35

qualitative data, analyzing 95 – 6
qualitative research, measurements 52 – 3

qualitative research methods 83 – 96
  case study method 87 – 93
    conducting 91 – 2
    preparation 89 – 90
    selection of cases 90 – 1
    types of case study design 92 – 3
  compared with quantitative 83, 84 Fig
  components 85
  data collection methods 95 Table
  group discussions 86, 87
  historical reviews 86, 87
  skills required 84
  triangulation 93 – 4
    definition 93
  types of 86
  when applicable 85 – 6
quantiles 151
quartiles 100, 151
questionnaires *see* surveys and questionnaires

random variable 145
  definition 145
  relationship between covariance and variance
    149 – 50
  sample 152
raw data 151
references, final report 138 – 9
reflective measurements 48
regression analysis,
  assumptions 113
  dummy variables 118 – 22
  see also linear regression analysis, simple;
    multiple regression analysis 315
rejection, errors of 155
rejection rule 155
reliability, sample 152
report *see* final report
research designs 14, 26 – 40
  causal 27, 29
  cause and effect 29 – 30
  choice of 26 – 7
  and choices 39 – 40
  classical experiment 31 – 3
  cross-sectional 35 – 7
  descriptive, description 27, 28 – 9
  exploratory, description 27, 28
  importance of theory 30 – 1
  one-shot case study 37 – 8
  and problem structure 27 – 9
  requirements 38 – 40
  time series 37

research designs (*continued*)
  validity threats 33−5
research and knowledge 15
research methodology 24−5
research orientations 8
research problems,
  structural 27
  unstructured 27
research problems, identifying and structuring
  11−13
research process 13−17
  conceptual (theoretical) level 15
  empirical level 15
  research before theory strategy 16, 17
  theory before research strategy 16−17
researcher, role of 6
row vector 150

sample,
  correlation coefficient 152
  describing 150−2
  dispersion matrix 152
  estimator 151
  reliability 152
  variance-covariance matrix 152
sampling 73−82, 152−3
  cluster sampling 79−80
  data matrix 76 Table
  definition 73
  distributions 152
  non-profitability sampling 74
  non-response 82
  parameters 75
  probability sampling 74
  sample size 76, 78, 80−2
    determination example 81
  simple random sampling,
    advantages and disadvantages 77
    worked example 74−7
  stratified random sampling 77−8
  systematic sampling 78−9
  target population 75
  variables 75
SAS 99
scales of measurement *see* measurements,
  levels
secondary data 53, 54−7
  advantages 55
  definition 54
  disadvantages 56−7
  sources 54−6
selection bias 34

semi-structured interviews 64−5, 89
sign test 107−8
simple random sampling,
  advantages and disadvantages 77
  worked example 74−7
simple regression 148
single case design 92, 93
specific factor 129
SPSS 99
square matrix 150
standard deviation 100
  designation 146
statistical conclusion validity 50
statistical hypothesis, definition 154
statistical inference,
  description 153
  principles of 153−6
statistical software packages 99
statistical terms 144
stimulus-response relationships 35
stratified random sampling 77−8
  compared with cluster sampling 79−80
structured interviews 65
structured problems 13
Student's *t*-distribution 100−1, 107, 146,
  152−3
Student's *t*-test statistic 156
survey research interviews 64
surveys and questionnaires 58−64
  analytical 59−60
  descriptive surveys 60
  guidelines for construction and wording of
    questionnaires 62−4
  length of questionnaires 61
  open-ended questions 61
  planning 59 Fig, 60−2
systematic sampling 78−9

t-based confidence interval 108
table of contents 133
tail probability 155
target population, case study method 90−1
test of homogeneity 105
test of independence 104, 105
theory,
  definition 19
  purpose 19
time series research designs 37
title page 133
total variance, definition 126
triangulation 93−4

two-sided alternative 155, 156

unbiased estimator of μ 152
unique factor 129
univariate frequency distribution 99
unpaired observations, data analysis 108−10
unstructured interviews 64
unstructured problems 13

validity 93
  threats 33−5
  types of 33
value chain 16−17
variables,
  definition 19, 75
  examining potential relationships 51

variables, dummy 118−22
  definition 118
  dependent 121−2
  independent 118−21
variables, independent 117
  orthogonal variables 117
  perfect multicollinearity 117
variance,
  designation 146
  one-way analysis 75, 109

weighted least squares 122
Wilcoxon confidence interval 101
Wilcoxon signed-rank test 108
written texts, analysis 53